SISTERS OF SACRED SONG

GARLAND REFERENCE LIBRARY
OF THE HUMANITIES
(VOL. 223)

Frontispiece to one of the hymn books issued for the charity children at Magdalen Chapel. From *Hymns Ancient and Modern. Historical Edition.* London: William Clowes and Sons, Ltd., 1909, p. xci.

SISTERS OF SACRED SONG
A Selected Listing of Women Hymnodists in Great Britain and America

Samuel J. Rogal

GARLAND PUBLISHING, INC. • NEW YORK & LONDON
1981

The photographs of Harriet Beecher Stowe and
Katharine Lee Bates are from THE GOSPEL IN
HYMNS—BACKGROUNDS AND INTERPRETA-
TIONS by Albert Edward Bailey. Copyright 1950 by
Charles Scribner's Sons. Reprinted by permission of
the publisher.

Library of Congress Cataloging in Publication Data

Rogal, Samuel J
  Sisters of sacred song.

  (Garland reference library of the humanities ;
v. 223)
  Bibliography: p.
  1. Women hymn writers—Great Britain. 2. Women
hymn writers—United States. I. Title.
BV325.R63   245'.21'0922   80-8482
ISBN 0-8240-9482-4

Printed on acid-free, 250-year-life paper
Manufactured in the United States of America

"It is plain from the history of all nations, that women cannot be confined to merely domestic pursuits, for they will not fulfil family duties, unless their minds take a wider range, and whilst they are kept in ignorance they become in the same proportion the slaves of pleasure as they are the slaves of man. Nor can they be shut out of great enterprises, though the narrowness of their minds often make them mar, what they are unable to comprehend."

Mary Wollstonecraft,
from *A Vindication of the Rights of Woman* (1792)

"I can never set myself to write verse. I believe my King suggests a thought and whispers me a musical line or two, and then I look up and thank Him delightedly, and go on with it. . . . The Master has not put a chest of poetic gold into my possession and said, 'Now use it as you like!' But He keeps the gold, and gives it me piece by piece just when He will and as much as He will, and no more."

Frances Ridley Havergal,
from *Letters* (1885)

CONTENTS

ILLUSTRATIONS

INTRODUCTION

The seeds of English congregational song were planted (in the form of paraphrases from the Psalms) in England late in the seventeenth century, nurtured by eighteenth-century Protestant Dissent and Nonconformity, and harvested—both in Britain and America—by the enthusiasm of nineteenth-century evangelicalism. Throughout those past centuries, from the psalter of Tate and Brady, through the true poetry of Watts, Doddridge, Charles Wesley, Cowper, and Newton, to the doctrinal control of *Hymns Ancient and Modern* and the electricity of Moody and Sankey, the hymnody of English-speaking people has maintained a distinct sense of catholicity. Few, indeed, are the hymns that have anchored themselves to specific sects or denominations; few, indeed, have been the hymnodists who have directed their lines to a particular volume of songs for public or private worship. Certainly, no one will deny the existence of a *Methodist* hymnal, a *Presbyterian* hymnal, a *Dutch Reformed* hymnal, an *Episcopal* hymnal, a *Christian Science* hymnal, a *Baptist* hymnal; but one would be hard pressed to define and to identify Episcopalian hymnody, to explicate the qualities of a purely Methodist hymn, to uncover Presbyterian doctrine in the hymnody of a poet positively identified as a Presbyterian. Instead, the majority of hymns written in English appear to have adjusted quite comfortably to a large variety of denominational mantles, while a poet known to hold membership in a particular religious body seems to have little or no difficulty skipping from the pages of one hymnal and coming to rest upon the surface of another.

If, then, the English hymn is to be considered *sectless*, it may also be termed *sexless*. For example, an historical survey of English congregational song will reveal, both in Great Britain and America, certain obvious thematic and occasional distinctions: there have been and still remain hymns for children, for marriage, for national and religious ceremonies, for holidays, for seasons, for specific doctrinal principles, and so on. However, there does not exist an easily identifiable body of hymnody that directs itself toward one sex or the other; nor do hymnologists generally distinguish between hymns written by men and those authored by women. In fact, it may be impossible even to begin to develop such a distinction. Observe, for instance, a single verse each from two separate hymns placed side by side:

1

Crowns and thorns may perish,
Kingdoms rise and wane,
But the Church of Jesus
Constant will remain;
Gates of hell can never
'Gainst that Church prevail;
We have Christ's own promise,
And that cannot fail.

2

He has sounded forth His trumpet
that shall never call retreat;
He is sifting out the hearts of men
before His judgment seat;
O be swift, my soul, to answer Him;
be jubilant my feet!
Our God is marching on.

Assuredly, within the contexts of form and substance, a number of critical issues relative to the two passages may be identified and developed; in the most general terms, we might even wish to set forth a discussion along pure theological lines. In other words, as poetry the two passages would be extended at least the superficial courtesies of critical commentary.

However, viewing the two passages in light of the sectless/ sexless argument, certain points are too obvious to ignore. Where lies the evidence, in the texts, that "Onward Christian Soldiers" was written by an *Anglican* and that "The Battle Hymn of the Republic" came from the mind and the heart of a *Unitarian?* Where is the clue that the first passage was written in 1864 and the second only two years previous? What tells us that the first example came from the vivid but disciplined imagination of a British male, the second from the fervor of an American female? In other words, where, among the crowns and the thorns and the constancy of the Christian Church do we find the Rev. Sabine Baring-Gould? Where, amidst the blasts of the trumpets and the shuffling of jubilant feet do we uncover Mrs. Julia Ward Howe? The answers, of course, focus on the inescapable fact that the hymn (as poem or as song), when placed before a congregation for consideration as an instrument of praise, tends to lose its historical and personal peculiarities. During the worship service, the hymn becomes, out of necessity, the property of that congregation, a vehicle for collective expression, for harmonious praise directed upward to God as creator and protector of human existence.

Because such matters as the hymnodist's sex, nationality, and denomination assume only slight significance, it is only fair to raise questions concerning the rationale for compiling a listing of *women* hymnodists of Britain and America. In terms of the arguments set forth in the preceding paragraphs, does not such a listing represent a contradiction? The exact response may easily be anticipated, especially if anyone takes the time to place the *hymn* (or religious ode) within the broad context of poetry, a context from which it most assuredly originates. Generally, the poetic contributions of British and American women, while not totally neglected, have, nevertheless, failed to receive sufficient critical attention and proper evaluation. There may exist a number of valid reasons for that lack of critical interest; but, principally, critical commentators and literary historians have tended to focus upon certain themes, directions, and trends in literature, being careful, always, to label writers and to place them in proper niches. Thus, a poet quickly becomes a neoclassicist, a romantic, a pre-Raphaelite, a transcendentalist, a Brahmin, a modern, an angry young man (never an angry young woman), a beat. Or, if none of those particular terms seem to fit, the critical commentator or literary historian can always fall back upon the sister discipline of history and label poets Augustans, Hanoverians, Victorians, Edwardians, colonials, post-moderns, or—if everything else fails—a lost generation.

Quite simply, an embarrassingly large number of poets who, initially, happened to be women and, secondarily, spent their poetic talents on religious verse failed to fit (easily or otherwise) into neat thematic or chronological molds of literary criticism. Although those women did not turn their heads entirely away from art, their fundamental concerns focused upon the conveyances (the congregational hymn) by which persons, in public or in private, could express the widest ranges of religious sentiment. More often than not, a particular vehicle sputtered and stalled until fueled by the notes from the right musical composition; only the proper mixture of words and melody would allow for the acceptance and eventual success of a poetic piece as a congregational hymn. In other words, the critical commentator may see signs of obvious weakness in the poetic armor of Mrs. Howe's "Mine eyes have seen the glory of the coming of the Lord"; but strap that poem securely to the back of William Steffe's "John Brown's body" tune, and it emerges as a classical expression of evangelical militancy, defiantly challenging any and all critical commentators to question its quality or its reasons for appeal.

Of course, the entire issue of poetic quality (which, in turn, determines *hymnodic* quality) versus popular appeal has always caused problems for critical commentators and hymnal editors alike. Simply, a congregational hymn (no matter from what sect or denomination it emerges) cannot stand alone upon those criteria applicable to pure poetry; by its very identity and being, the congregational hymn must serve the theological, liturgical, and even national interests of a wide variety of worshipers. Thus, the results, when viewed within the contents of several hymnals, do not always find the highest levels of poetic quality. In other words, consistency of merit has never really been a pronounced characteristic of hymnodic expression—either in Britain or America, either among male or female hymn writers. Further, the female hymnodists on both sides of the Atlantic Ocean have seemed, since the eighteenth century, not always conscious of whether they could or should hold congregational song to a consistent course of literary merit. Such an observation does not necessarily condemn those women who limited their literary activity to the writing of congregational poems; rather, such an observation underscores the extent to which the "Sisters of Sacred Song" listed herein reacted, as best they could, to the specific needs of their audiences.

Consider, first, the *high ground* of hymnodic expression, the attempt of the poet to produce a highly literary hymnodic piece. Certainly, near the top of the list of this category—in fact, it may rank with the finest pieces of devotional poetry in English—is

Charlotte Elliott's "Just as I am, without one plea," a poem published, initially, in the *Invalid's Hymn Book* (1836). It reads, in
part:

> 1. Just as I am, without one plea,
>   But that Thy blood was shed for me,
>   And that Thou bidd'st me come to Thee,
>   O Lamb of God, I come.
>
> . . . .
>
> 4. Just as I am, poor, wretched, blind;
>   Sight, riches, healing of the mind,
>   Yea, all I need, in Thee to find,
>   O Lamb of God, I come.
>
> . . . .
>
> 6. Just as I am, Thy love unknown
>   Has broken every barrier down;
>   Now to be Thine, yea, Thine alone,
>   O Lamb of God, I come.

The language of those lines—simple, direct, sincere—fits easily
the overall purpose of the hymn: a tender dedicatory ode to
those suffering from physical illness or spiritual infirmity. Of
course, that Miss Elliott spent the last fifty years of her life as an
invalid allowed her hymns to be framed within the proper limits
of sincerity and carefully controlled emotion. She convinces her
readers and singers, and she certainly moves them, but she does
not try to intimidate them with her own tears.

One other example of the poet's attempt to achieve a high
literary level and still serve the needs of a congregation at worship is
seen in Dorothy Gurney's hymn for holy matrimony, "O perfect
Love, all human thought transcending" (1883), cited below in full:

> 1. O perfect Love, all human thought
>   transcending,
>   Lowly we kneel in prayer before Thy
>   throne,

That theirs may be the love that knows no
    ending,
    Whom Thou for ever more dost join in
      one.

2. O perfect Life, be Thou their full
      assurance
    Of tender charity and steadfast faith,
Of patient hope, and quiet, brave
      endurance,
    With childlike trust that fears not pain
      nor death.

3. Grant them the joy which brightens
      earthly sorrow;
    Grant them the peace which calms all
      earthly strife,
And to life's day the glorious unknown
      morrow
    That dawns upon eternal love and life.

In much the same manner as the Elliott hymn, the above lines of
Miss Gurney provide a backdrop of obvious dignity for one of
the most meaningful of religious ceremonies. There is nothing
at all complicated or elaborate about the language, which allows
the poem to be set to music without any disadvantage to the
sense of the text. In regard to congregational song, to the actual
relationship between hymn and worship service, one cannot
really demand much more than what Gurney actually produced.

However, if hymnody can rise to the heights of poetic compe-
tence, it can also plunge into the deepest caverns of mediocrity.
Seemingly, the efforts of Charlotte Elliott and Dorothy Gurney
to clothe congregational song in the mantle of literary re-
spectability were challenged, beginning about the middle of the
nineteenth century, by the exponents of popularism and out-
right evangelical fervor. The journey from such pieces as "Just
as I am" and "O perfect Love, all human thought transcending"
to the likes of Priscilla Owens' "Will your anchor hold" is, indeed, a descent into the farthest corners of poetic discomfort:

1. Will your anchor hold in the storms of
        life,
    When the clouds unfold their wings of
        strife?
    When the strong tides lift, and the cables
        strain,
    Will your anchor drift, or firm remain?

    Refrain:
    We have an anchor that keeps the soul
    Steadfast and sure while the billows roll,
    Fastened to the Rock which cannot move,
    Grounded firm and deep in the Saviour's
        love.

2. It is safely moored, 'twill the storm
        withstand,
    For 'tis well secured by the Saviour's
        hand;
    Though the tempest rage and the wild
        winds blow,
    Not an angry wave shall our bark
        o'er-flow.

3. When our eyes behold through the
        gathering night
    The city of gold, our harbor bright,
    We shall anchor fast by the heavenly
        shore,
    With the storms all past forever more.

The tired and trite imagery of the lines hardly requires explica-
tion. All that needs saying is that the entire poem functions as a
medium through which *singers* can quickly and easily find a
channel through which to thrust their most profound but im-
mediate religious emotions. As such, the *written* language of the
piece gives way almost totally to whatever *musical* language hap-
pens to carry it along. Nonetheless, the real value of such gospel
songs to the student of hymnology focuses upon the specifics of

how and why a hymn, a poem of deep religious significance or an ode directed to a divine being, differs from the popular gospel song, of which the Owens piece is an outstanding example.

The gospel song, as an effective instrument for the expression of evangelical zeal, even permitted certain female versifiers to cultivate their talents as writers of verse *and* music. Thus, such practitioners as Mrs. Mary Stanley Bounce Dana proved herself a true "Sister of Sacred Song" with this effort:

> 1. Flee as a bird to your mountain,
>   Thou who art weary of sin;
>   Go to the clear, flowing fountain,
>   Where you may wish to be clean;
>   Fly, for th' Avenger is near thee;
>   Call, and the Saviour will hear thee;
>   He on his bosom will bear thee,
>   Thou who art weary of sin,
>   O thou who art weary of sin.
>
> 2. He is the bountiful Giver,
>   Now unto Him draw near;
>   Peace then shall flow like a river,
>   Thou shalt be saved from thy fear.
>   Hark! 'tis the Saviour calling!
>   Haste! for the twilight is falling!
>   Flee, for the night is appalling!
>   And thou shalt be saved from thy fear,
>   And thou shalt be saved from thy fear.

Two more stanzas follow, but they do no more or no less damage to the poetic senses than those cited above. The staccato of sharp commands—*flee, go, fly, call, hark, haste*—combined with the overabundance of rhythm—*calling, falling, appalling,* for instance—literally drives the mind away from the sense of the piece, leaving the worshipers with no other choice but to sing loudly, tap their fingers against their hymnals, and hope for the best.

Between the high, temperate ground of the literary hymn and the heat of the gospel song lies a large body of congregational hymnody that, if nothing else can be said of it, seems generally not to offend the intellects and the spirits of either of the two extremes. For that reason, the so-called middle ground of congregational song appears to be the most popular; that is, the hymns within this category tend to have taken up lengthy periods of residence in a large number of hymnals which, in turn, represent a wide range of denominations. In fact, two of them may be found side by side (#187, #188) in the 1966 *Methodist Hymnal* and only pages apart (#284, #310) in the 1955 *Hymnal* of the Presbyterian Church. The first, by Frances Havergal, reads, in part,

> 1. Take my life, and let it be
>   Consecrated, Lord to Thee.
>   Take my moments and my days;
>   Let them flow in ceaseless praise.
>   Take my hands, and let them move
>   At the impulse of Thy love.
>   Take my feet and let them be,
>   Swift and beautiful for Thee.

Lucy Larcom's opening stanza on a similar theme illustrates the connection between the two poems:

> 1. Draw Thou my soul, O Christ,
>   Closer to Thine;
>   Breathe into every wish
>   Thy will divine!
>   Raise my low self above,
>   Won by Thy deathless love;
>   Ever, O Christ, through mine,
>   Let Thy life shine.

Certainly, both hymns have reaped the benefits of musical compositions of the highest quality: the music to the Havergal piece by the eminent French operatic composer Louis Joseph Ferdinand Herold; the tune for the Larcom hymn by Arthur Seymour Sullivan. Nonetheless, the poetry in both remains palat-

able. Miss Havergal may indeed choose to begin half of her two
dozen lines with the word *Take*; but that imperative verb serves
as her thesis, not simply (as in the gospel song) for the purpose
of force-feeding her singers with rhythm. For the same
reason—emphasis of theme—Miss Larcom asks God to *draw*,
lead, *breathe*, *lift*, *raise*, and *cleanse*. In each poem, the worshiper
has the opportunity to commit both mind and heart to the praise
of God; in each poem, the hymnodist achieves a balance between
reason and emotion, insuring, in turn, that the hymn holds firm
to its proper place and perspective within the scheme and the
scope of the worship service.

Although the majority of British and American hymns can
be placed easily into the three broad categories of overall hymnodic quality previously discussed, students of hymnology
should recognize, in addition, at least three very specific types of
congregational song to which female hymnodists have tra-
ditionally contributed. These may be identified as (1) the national hymn, (2) the children's hymn, and (3) the hymn as
prayer. Undoubtedly, the most recognizable among the national
hymns is that authored by Katharine Lee Bates in 1893:

1. O beautiful for spacious skies, for amber
       waves of grain,
    For purple mountain majesties above the
       fruited plain!
    America! America! God shed his grace on
       thee,
    And crown thy good with brotherhood
    From sea to shining sea.

    . . . .

3. O beautiful for heroes proved in
       liberating strife,
    Who more than self their country loved,
       and mercy more than life!
    America! America! May God thy gold
       refine,
    Till all success be nobleness, and every
       gain devine.

In terms of her poetry, Miss Bates provided the proper combination of fundamental scriptural doctrine and equally spontaneous nationalistic emotion: the natural setting of a God-created universe still allows room for the success and the nobility of God's creatures—specifically, man. The hymn itself, because of that combination, does not have to lean heavily upon Samuel Ward's music to convey its religious-patriotic thesis. Indeed, even without Ward's contribution, the piece still ranks high among that fading group of poems intended—on extremely special and rare occasions—to strike at the conscience of a nation, to draw forth the rhetorical reverberations of national pride.

Children's hymnody, which gained recognition early in the eighteenth century (particularly in Germany and England), has suffered by association and mistaken identity. For example, the English-speaking nations have labored under the heavily moralistic "busy little bee" style of Isaac Watts, while male hymnodists early turned the responsibility for writing hymns to and about children to their female colleagues. However, the difficulty has not been with the writers, but rather with the audience and the subject, as hymnodists have felt that to reach the minds and the hearts of children, they must necessarily produce trite and extremely simplistic poetry. Despite the molds into which the form has been cast, certain poets have demonstrated that children's hymnody can be carried forward with maturity and dignity. Consider, for example, Catherine Winkworth's translation of Johann Wilhelm Meinhold's "Guter Hirt, du hast gestillt":

1. Gentle Shepherd, Thou hast still'd
   Now Thy little lamb's brief weeping:
   Ah, how peaceful, pale, and mild
   In its narrowed bed 'tis sleeping!
   And no sigh of anguish sore
   Heaves that little bosom more.

2. In this world of care and pain,
   Lord, Thou wouldst no longer leave it;
   To the sunny heavenly plain
   Thou dost now with joy receive it;

> Clothed in robes of spotless white,
> Now it dwells with Thee in light.

3. Ah, Lord Jesus, grant that we
   Where it lives may soon be living,
   And the lovely pastures see
   That its heavenly food are giving;
   Then the gain of death we prove,
   Though Thou take what most we love.

The hymn rises above the usual maudlin reaction to childhood death, and it also holds the fiats of moral instruction to a minimum. As a skilled translator and versifier, Miss Winkworth easily found the middle ground between Meinhold's stoicism, seasoned with her own tendency toward Anglican indifference, and "the-roll-is-called-up-yonder" school advocated by less restrained exponents of the evangelical revival.

Finally, there exists the need to consider the function of the hymn as a form of universal prayer, in which the hymnodist attempts to provide a vehicle for the collective thoughts of an entire congregation. An obvious illustration may be formed from three stanzas of Adelaide Procter's "evening" hymn:

1. The shadows of the evening hours
   Fall from the darkening sky;
   Upon the fragrance of the flowers
   The dews of evening lie.
   Before Thy throne, O Lord of heaven,
   We kneel at close of day;
   Look on Thy children from on high,
   And hear us while we pray.

2. The sorrows of Thy servants, Lord,
   O do not Thy despise,
   But let the incense of our prayers
   Before Thy mercy rise.
   The brightness of the coming night
   Upon the darkness rolls;
   With hopes of future glory chase
   The shadows on our souls.

3. Slowly the rays of daylight fade:
     So fade within our heart
    The hope in earthly love and joy,
     That one by one depart.
    Slowly the bright stars, one by one,
     Within the heavens shine:
    Give us, O Lord, fresh hopes in heaven,
     And trust in things divine.

Miss Procter is a true daughter of theological tradition, and her sense of symmetry—natural, theological, and poetic—allows her to explicate, with utmost clarity, man's role within God's universal frame. Thus, in the final stanza, her hymnodic prayer reaches the obvious conclusion:

     Give us a respite from our toil;
      Calm and subdue our woes;
     Through the long day we labour, Lord
      O give us now repose.

What begins to emerge, then, is the idea that by its very direction and intention, hymnody requires a commitment to and a drawing away from art—or from poetry. The hymn writers (male *and* female) in Britain and America, from the early eighteenth century to the present, have been forced to divide themselves and their poetry between art and the requisites of practical worship. Such division of intellectual and emotional labor had little effect upon the male hymnodists, since the vast majority came from, belonged to, and officially served the Church. As clerics, they remained abreast of their congregations' hymnodic needs; in fact, in certain instances (Isaac Watts, the Wesleys, Joseph Priestley, James Martineau, Harry Emerson Fosdick), they were in positions to determine and even to control those needs. Their female counterparts, however, generally had no such freedom or influence. Without office or status, they were (especially during the eighteenth and nineteenth centuries) forced to ride the trends established by their then acknowledged physical and intellectual superiors. Unfortunately, a considerable number of female hymnodists, as well as a large number of their hymns, never really found the opportunity even to begin the struggle for congregational acceptance.

The main purpose of this list, therefore, is to chart the course that will lead, eventually, to a recognition of the *totality* of women's contributions to the history and development of British and American congregational song. Certainly, there remains much exploration for scholars within the general area of hymnology; concerning the role of women in that field, *everything* remains to be explored! Thus, the listing of names, dates, titles, and national and denominational identity will, it is hoped, serve as the initial step toward confrontation of what seems to be a valid critical point: that hymnody demonstrates the degree to which a significant number of British and American women, from the early eighteenth century to the present, have clearly manifested their Christian piety and, at the same time, have made notable contributions to poetry in English.

EXPLANATION OF THE LIST

Entries are arranged alphabetically, by author's last name. In cases of marriage, the husband's name becomes the key to identification. As far as possible, all known names are indicated, as *VAN ALSTYNE, Frances Jane Crosby.* Then, for each entry (as far as possible), the following information appears:

1. Dates of birth and death
2. National identity
3. Denominational identity
4. Hymnals and hymn collections edited *principally* by the writer, with dates of publication, listed alphabetically by title
5. The most widely accepted (in congregational use) titles of hymns by the author, followed (in parentheses) by the date of publication in a hymn collection or volume of poetry (whichever comes first); items arranged al-

phabetically by first-line title ("Mine eyes have seen the glory . . ." rather than *The Battle Hymn of the Republic*). If two dates appear, the *first* indicates the year in which the hymn was *written*.

6. An asterisk (*) preceding a hymn title indicates that the piece is a *translation* from another language. The dates that follow refer to the publication of the hymn in English.

7. As is the general practice in hymnology, all hymns contained herein are identified by the opening line of the first verse.

Unfortunately, biographical information on each and every writer in this list is not easy to come by. Certain hymnodists herein are, quite frankly, obscure literary figures; others are simply too contemporary, and thus do not appear in the most recent biographical reference works. The forthcoming *Dictionary of American Hymnology*, sponsored by the Hymn Society of America, and some future updating of Julian's *Dictionary of Hymnology* may fill some needed gaps. Until then, one is left to the excruciatingly slow process of scanning scores of hymnals and hymn collections—a task that bears too little fruit for the labor involved.

SOURCES

The following works were consulted in the preparation of this listing:

Barkley, John M. (ed.). HANDBOOK TO THE CHURCH HYMNARY, 3rd. ed. London: Oxford University Press, 1979.

Benson, Louis Fitzgerald. THE ENGLISH HYMN. ITS DEVELOPMENT AND USE IN WORSHIP. 1915; rpt. Richmond, Virginia: John Knox Press, 1962.

Bickersteth, Edward Henry (ed.). THE HYMNAL COMPAN-
ION TO THE BOOK OF COMMON PRAYER, 3rd. ed.,
rev. London: Longman's, Green and Company, 1890.
THE BROADMAN HYMNAL. Nashville, Tennessee: The
Broadman Press, 1940.
Covert, William Chalmers, and Calvin Weiss Laufer (eds.).
HANDBOOK TO THE HYMNAL. Philadelphia: Presbyte-
rian Board of Christian Education, 1936.
Dickinson, Clarence, and Calvin Weiss Laufer (eds.). THE
HYMNAL ... OF THE PRESBYTERIAN CHURCH IN
THE UNITED STATES OF AMERICA. Philadelphia:
Presbyterian Board of Christian Education, 1937.
Diehl, Katharine Smith. HYMNS AND TUNES—AN INDEX.
New York and London: The Scarecrow Press, 1966.
Fairchild, Hoxie Neale. RELIGIOUS TRENDS IN ENGLISH
POETRY. 6 vols. New York and London: Columbia Univer-
sity Press, 1939–1968.
Foote, Henry Wilder. THREE CENTURIES OF AMERICAN
HYMNODY. 1940; rpt. New York: Archon Books, 1968.
Higginson, J. Vincent. HANDBOOK FOR AMERICAN
CATHOLIC HYMNALS. New York: The Hymn Society of
America, 1975.
HYMNAL AND LITURGIES OF THE MORAVIAN
CHURCH. Bethlehem, Pennsylvania: Provincial Synod,
1920.
THE HYMNAL, AS AUTHORIZED ... BY ... THE PROT-
ESTANT EPISCOPAL CHURCH IN THE UNITED
STATES. New York: The Church Pension Fund, 1933.
HYMNAL FOR CHRISTIAN WORSHIP. Richmond, Virginia:
John Knox Press, 1940.
HYMNAL OF THE METHODIST EPISCOPAL CHURCH,
WITH TUNES. New York: Phillips and Hunt, 1887.
HYMNAL OF THE METHODIST EPISCOPAL CHURCH,
WITH TUNES. New York: Hunt and Eaton, 1889.
THE HYMNBOOK. PUBLISHED BY PRESBYTERIAN
CHURCH IN THE UNITED STATES, THE UNITED
PRESBYTERIAN CHURCH IN THE U.S.A., REFORMED

CHURCH IN AMERICA. Richmond, Philadelphia, New York: [John Knox Press,] 1955.

HYMNS ANCIENT AND MODERN. FOR USE IN THE SERVICES OF THE CHURCH. WITH ACCOMPANYING TUNES. HISTORICAL EDITION. London: William Clowes and Sons, Limited, 1909.

HYMNS FOR THE '70's. New York: The Hymn Society of America, 1971.

HYMNS OF HOPE. New York: The Hymn Society of America, 1971.

Jepson, Harry B., and Charles R. Brown (eds.). UNIVERSITY HYMNS. New Haven: Yale University Press, 1924.

Julian, John (ed.). A DICTIONARY OF HYMNOLOGY, 2nd. ed., rev. 2 vols. 1907; rpt. New York: Dover Publications, Inc., 1957.

McDormand, Thomas B., and Frederic S. Crossman. JUDSON CONCORDANCE TO HYMNS. Valley Forge, Pennsylvania: The Judson Press, 1965.

THE METHODIST HYMNAL. New York: Eaton and Mains, 1905.

THE METHODIST HYMNAL. New York: The Methodist Book Concern, 1935.

THE METHODIST HYMNAL. Nashville, Tennessee: The Methodist Publishing House, 1966.

NEW HYMNS FOR AMERICA, 1976. New York: The Hymn Society of America, 1975.

NEW HYMNS ON AGING AND THE LATER YEARS. Springfield, Ohio, and Washington, D.C.: The Hymn Society of America and National Retired Teachers Association/American Association of Retired Persons, 1976.

Northcott, Cecil. HYMNS IN CHRISTIAN WORSHIP. Richmond, Virginia: John Knox Press, 1964.

THE NORTHFIELD AND MOUNT HERMON HYMNAL. Northfield, Massachusetts: Northfield and Mount Hermon Schools, 1964.

PSALMS AND HYMNS, WITH THE DOCTRINAL STANDARDS AND LITURGY OF THE REFORMED

PROTESTANT DUTCH CHURCH. Philadelphia: Printed by Ferguson Brothers and Company, 1887.

Routley, Erik. HYMNS TODAY AND TOMORROW. Nashville, Tennessee: Abingdon Press, 1964.

SIXTY HYMNS FROM *SONGS OF ZION*. A HYMNAL SUPPLEMENT. Whittier, California: Praise Publications, Inc., 1977.

SONGS AND HYMNS FOR PRIMARY CHILDREN. Philadelphia: The Westminster Press, 1963.

Women Hymnodists
in Great Britain and America

Titles preceded by an asterisk (*) are translations.

ADAMS, Jessie (1866-1954). British. Quaker

I feel the winds of God today (1907)

ADAMS, Sarah Flower (1805-1848). British. Unitarian

*The Flock at the Fountain. A Catechism and Hymns for
   Children* (1845)

Creator, Spirit! Thou the first (1841)
Darkness shrouded Calvary (1841)
Gently fall the dews of eve (1841)
Go and watch the autumn leaves (1841)
He sendeth sun, He sendeth shower (1841)
Living or dying, Lord, I would be Thine (1841)
Nearer, my God, to Thee (1841)
O hallowed memories of the past (1841)
O human heart! thou hast a song (1841)
O I would sing a song of praise (1841)
O Love! thou makest all things even (1841)
Part in peace! Christ's life was peace (1841)
Part in peace! is day before us? (1841)
Sing to the Lord! for His mercies are sure (1841)
The mourners came at break of day (1841)

AGNEW, Edith (b. 1897). American. Presbyterian

There is no cradle ready (1944)
When Jesus saw the fishermen (1953)

AIRD, Marion Paul (1815-1888). Scottish. Presbyterian

Had I the wings of a dove, I would fly (1853)

AKERMAN, Lucy Evelina Metcalf (1816-1874). American. Unitar-
    ian

    Nothing but leaves, the Spirit grieves (1858)

ALDERSON, Eliza Sibbald Dykes (1818-1889). British. Church
    of England

    And now, beloved Lord, Thy soul resigning (1868)
    Lord of glory, Who hast bought us (1864, 1868)

ALEXANDER, Cecil Frances Humphreys (1823-1895). Irish. United
    Church of England

    Hymns Descriptive and Devotional (1858)
    Hymns for Little Children (1848)
    Moral Songs (n.d.)
    Narrative Hymns for Village Schools (1853)

    All things bright and beautiful (1848)
    Beyond the wicked city walls (1859)
    Christ has ascended up again (1853)
    Christian children must be holy (1853)
    Dead is thy daughter; trouble not the Master (1865)
    Dear Lord, on this Thy servant's day (1875)
    Do no sinful action (1848)
    Every morning the red sun (1848)
    For all Thy Saints, a noble throng (1875)
    Forgive them, O my Father (1875)
    Forsaken once, and thrice denied (1875)
    From out the clouds of amber light (1875)
    He cometh on yon hallowed Board (1865)
    He is coming, He is coming (1858)
    He is risen! He is risen! tell it with a joyful sound (1846)
    His are the thousand sparkling rills (1875)
    How good is the Almighty God (1848)
    In the rich man's garden (1853)
    It was early in the morning (1853)
    Jesus calls us; o'er the tumult (1852)
    Light of the world that shines to bless (1858)
    O Jesus bruised and wounded more (1859)
    Once in royal David's city (1848)
    Pain and toil are over now (1846)
    Saw you never in the twilight (1853)
    So be it, Lord, the prayers are prayed (1848)
    Souls in heathen darkness lying (1851)
    Spirit of God, that moved of old (1852)
    Still bright and blue doth Jordan flow (1853)

Cecil Frances Alexander. From *Hymns Ancient and Modern. Historical Edition*. London: William Clowes and Sons, Ltd., 1909, p. cvii. "From a photograph by Elliott and Fry"

The angels stand around Thy throne (1848)
The eternal gates lift up their heads (1852)
The faithful men of every land (1848)
The golden gates are lifted up (1858)
The roseate hues of early dawn (1852)
The saints of God are holy men (1848)
The sick man in his chamber (1859)
The wise men to Thy cradle throne (1858)
There is a green hill far away (1848)
There is one way, only one (1875)
Up in heaven, up in heaven (1848)
We are but little children poor (1850)
We are little Christian children (1848)
We were washed in holy water (1848)
When of old the Jewish mothers (1853)
When the churchyard side by side (1848)
When wounded sore the stricken soul (1858)

ANDERSON, Maria Frances (b. 1819). American (b. Paris, France).
    Baptist

    Our country's voice is pleading (1849)

ARMITAGE, Ella Sophia Bulley (1841-1931). British. Congrega-
    tional

    The Garden of the Lord (1881)

    Except the Lord the temple built (1875, 1881)
    External love, whose law doth sway (1879, 1881)
    It is the Lord Himself who fends (1881)
    March on, march on, ye soldiers true (1886)
    Not only for the goodly fruit-trees fall (1881)
    O Father, in Thy Father's heart (1887)
    O Lord of all, we bring to Thee (1879, 1881)
    O Lord of hosts, the fight is long (1894)
    O Lord of life, and love, and power (1875, 1881)
    Our dear Lord's garden (1881)
    Praise for the Garden of God upon earth (1881)
    The day of prayer is ending (1894)
    Though home be dear, and life be sweet (1894)

ARMSTRONG, Florence Catherine (b. 1843). Irish

    O to be over yonder (1862, 1865)

ASHLEY, Mrs. Edmund

> *Let me go, let me go, Jesus, face to face, to know (1867)
> *My soul adores the might of loving (1867)

AUBER, Harriet (1773-1862). British. Church of England

> *The Spirit of the Psalms* (1829)

> Arise, ye people, and adore (1829)
> As Thy chosen people, Lord (1829)
> Bright was the guiding star that led (1829)
> Can guilty man indeed believe (1829)
> Delightful is the task to sing (1829)
> Ere mountains reared their forms sublime (1829)
> Father of spirits, nature's God (1829)
> Great God, wert Thou extreme to mark (1829)
> Hail, all hail, the joyful morn (1829)
> Hasten, Lord, the glorious time (1829)
> How blest are they who daily prove (1829)
> How blest the children of the Lord (1829)
> Jehovah, great and awful name (1829)
> Jehovah reigns, O earth rejoice (1829)
> Jesus, Lord, to Thee we sing (1829)
> Join, all ye servants of the Lord (1829)
> O all ye lands, rejoice in God (1829)
> O God our strength, to Thee the song (1829)
> O praise our great and gracious Lord (1829)
> O Thou Whom heaven's bright host revere (1829)
> On Thy Church, O power divine (1829)
> Our blest Redeemer, ere He breathed (1829)
> Praise the Lord, our mighty King (1829)
> Spirit of Peace, who as a dove (1829)
> Sweet is the work, O Lord (1829)
> That Thou, O Lord, art ever nigh (1829)
> The Lord, Who hath redeemed our souls (1829)
> Thou by whose strength the mountains stand (1829)
> To heaven our longing eyes we raise (1829)
> Vainly through night's weary hours (1829)
> Vainly through the night the danger (1829)
> When all bespeaks a father's love (1829)
> When dangers press and fears invade (1829)
> While all the golden harps above (1829)
> Who, O Lord, when life is o'er (1829)
> Whom have we, Lord, in heaven, but Thee (1829)
> Wide, ye heavenly gates, unfold (1829)
> With hearts in love abounding (1829)
> With joy we hail the sacred day (1829)

BACHE, Sarah (1771-1844). British. Unitarian

   "See how he loved," exclaimed the Jews (1812)

BAILLIE, Joanna (1762-1851). Scottish. Presbyterian

   Clothed in majesty sublime (1840)

BAKER, Amy Susan Margaret (b. 1847). British. Church of
      England

   Hymns and Songs for Festivals and Other Occasions (1876)
   Lays for the Little Ones (1876)

   True friends help each other (1876)
   We are only little workers (1876)

BAKER, Mary A. American. Baptist

   Master, the tempest is raging (1874)
   Why perish with cold and with hunger? (1881)

BALFOUR, Clara Liddell Lucas (1808-1878). British

   Come, gentle daughters of our land (n.d.)

BALLARD, Dorothy

   Give praise to God who made the day (1959)
   Glad welcome to the morning (1959)
   God has made the changing seasons (1959)
   I believe in Jesus (1960)
   In the crowds that came to Jesus (1959)
   Jesus Christ is risen (1960)
   The Bible tells how sky and sea (1959)

BANCROFT, Charitie Lees Smith (1841-1923). Irish. United
      Church of England and Ireland

   Before the throne of God above (1863)
   Lord, I desire to live as one (1861)
   O for the robes of whiteness (1860)
   The King of glory standeth (1867)

BARBAULD, Anna Laetitia Aiken (1743-1825).   British.   Independent, Unitarian

Hymns in Prose for Children (1781)

Again the Lord of life and light (1772)
Awake, my soul, lift up thine eyes (1772)
Behold, where breathing love divine (1772)
Come, said Jesus' sacred voice (1792)
God of my life, and author of my days (1772, 1773)
How blest the sacred tie that binds (1792)
How may earth and heaven unite (1807)
Jehovah reigns, let every nation hear (1772)
Joy to the followers of the Lord (1820, 1825)
Lo, where a crowd of pilgrims toll (1792)
Our country is Immanuel's ground (1792)
Praise to God, immortal praise (1772)
Pure spirit, O where art thou now? (1808, 1825)
Salt of the earth, ye virtuous few (1825)
Sleep, sleep to-day, tormenting cares (1807)
Sweet is the scene when virtue dies (1809)
When as returns the solemn day (1807)
When life as opening buds is sweet (1814)

BARNARD, Winifred Eva (b. 1892).   British.   Church of England

Let us sing our song of praise (1947)

BATES, Katharine Lee (1859-1929).   American

Dear God, our Father, at Thy knee confessing (1928)
O beautiful for spacious skies (1893, 1899)
The Kings of the East are riding (n.d.)

BAXTER, Lydia (1809-1874).   American.   Baptist

Cast thy net again, my brother (1873)
Go, work in my vineyard (1873)
I'm kneeling, Lord, at mercy's gate (1879)
I'm weary, I'm fainting, my day's work is done (1873)
In the fadeless spring-time (1872, 1873)
One by one we cross the river (1866)
Take the name of Jesus with you (1870, 1871)
The Master is coming (1870)
There is a gate that stands ajar (1872, 1874)

Katharine Lee Bates. From Albert Edward Bailey. *The Gospel in Hymns. Backgrounds and Interpretations.* New York: Charles Scribner's Sons, 1950, p. 567.

BEALE, Mary Craddock (1632-1697). British. Church of England

   Paraphrases of Psalms 13, 52, 70, and 130 (1667)

BECHTEL, Helen G.

   Happy is the nation whose God is the Lord (1959)
   Never forget what God has done (1959)
   O come with joy and worship God (1959)

BEVAN, Emma Frances Shuttleworth (1827-1909). British. Church
    of England

   Songs of Eternal Life, trans. from the German (1858)
   Songs of Praise for Christian Pilgrims (1859)

   *All fair within those children of the light (1858)
   *From thy glorious heaven (1859)
   *Give glory to the Son of God (1858)
   *Glorious are the fields of heaven (1859)
   *How many stars are shining (1859)
   *I go from grief and sighing (1858)
   *In faith we sing this song of thankfulness (1858)
   *In Jesus' arms her soul doth rest (1858)
   *Is God for me? I fear not (1858)
   *Jerusalem! thou glorious city-height (1858)
   *Little children, God above (1858)
   *My soul hath found the steadfast ground (1858)
   *Now I close my tired eyes (1859)
   *O fire of love, what earthly words (1858)
   *O God, O Spirit, Light of life (1858)
   *O how sweet it is to pray (1859)
   *O how sweet the wondrous story (1859)
   *O what joy for them is stored (1858)
   *Oh! could I but be still (1859)
   *Rise, ye children of salvation (1858)
   *Should I not be meek and still (1858)
   *Sinners Jesus will receive (1858)
   *Something every heart is loving (1858)
   *The day is gone; my soul looks on (1858)
   *There is a day of rest before thee (1858)
   *Thou sweet beloved will of God (1858)
   *Thou who breakest every fetter (1858)
   *Waken! from the tower it soundeth (1858)
   *Wearily my spirit speaketh (1858)

BLACK, Mary Anne Manning (1855–1882). British. Church of
      England

   There's a fold, both safe and happy (1878, 1880)

BODE, Alice Mary (b. 1847). British. Church of England

   Once pledged by the Cross (1901)

BONAR, Jane Catharine Lundie (1821–1884). Scottish. Free
      Church of Scotland (Presbyterian)

   Pass away, earthly joy (1844)

BORTHWICK, Jane Laurie (1813–1897). Scottish. Presbyterian

   Hymns from the Land of Luther, from the German, with Sarah
      Borthwick Findlater. First series, 1854; 2nd. ser.,
      1855; 3rd. ser., 1858; 4th ser., 1862.

   *A few more conflicts, toils, and tears (1875)
   *A gentle angel walketh (1855)
   *A little while! so spake our gracious Lord (1858)
   *A pilgrim and a stranger (1858)
   *All things are yours! O sweet message of mercy divine (1855)
   *As Thou wilt, my God! I ever say (1858)
   *At last, all shall be well with those His own (1858)
   *Be still my soul! the Lord is on thy side (1855)
   *Beloved and honoured, fare thee well (1858)
   *Breezes of spring, all earth to life awaking (1862)
   *Christ, my Lord, is all my hope (1864)
   *Come at the morning hour (1862)
   *Come forth! Come on, with solemn song (1855)
    Come, labour on (1859)
   *Commit thou every sorrow, And care (1864)
   *Dark, mighty ocean, rolling to our feet (1858)
   *Darkness reigns—the hum of life's commotion (1854)
   *Dear to Thee, O Lord, and precious (1875)
   *Depart, my child (1854)
   *Give thanks for all things, children of your God (1875)
   *Hallelujah! fairest morning (1858)
   *Hallelujah! I believe! (1858)
   *Hallelujah! Jesus lives! (1862)
   *He, Who the living God hath chosen (1864)
   *Hear me, my friends! the hour has come (1858)
   *Holy Comforter divine (1864)
   *How blessed, from the bonds of sin (1854)

*How brightly shines the morning star (1864)
 I do not doubt Thy wise and holy will (1859)
*I had once four lovely children (1862)
*I journey forth rejoicing (1854)
*I rest with Thee, Lord! whither should I go (1855)
*If only he is mine (1855)
*Is Thy work all ended, Lord? (1862)
*Jesus' hour is not yet come (1855)
*Jesus in bonds of death had lain (1864)
*Jesus shall lead on (1846)
*Jesus, sun of righteousness (1855)
*Long hast thou wept and sorrowed (1862)
 Lord, Thou knowest all the weakness (1859)
*Love and a Cross together blest (1862)
*Low at Thy feet my spirit lies (1875)
*My Jesus, as Thou wilt (1854)
*My soul, thy great Redeemer see (1864)
*Never couldst Thou bear to grieve us (1854)
*Now awake my soul, my senses (1864)
*Now I find a lasting joy (1864)
*Now, in peace of God (1875)
*O Christ, my life, my Saviour (1875)
*O everlasting source of life and light (1862)
*O great and gracious God (1864)
*O my heart, be calm and patient (1864)
*O sweet home echo on the pilgrim's way (1858)
*Oh! how blessed are ye, saints forgiven (1854)
*Once a merchant travelled far and wide (1855)
*Peace, be still, through the night (1875)
*Praise to Jehovah! the Almighty the King of Creation (1855)
 Rejoice, my fellow pilgrim (1859)
*Remember me, my God! remember me! (1854)
 Rest, weary heart: the penalty is borne (1859)
 Rest, weary soul (1864)
*Return! return! poor long-lost wanderer, home (1855)
*Saviour of sinners, now revive us (1864)
*Soul, arise, dispel thy sadness (1864)
*Still on the shores of home my feet are standing (1862)
*Sun of comfort, art Thou fled for ever (1855)
*Tell me not of earthly love (1862)
*The day departs, my soul and heart (1861)
*This is the day the Lord hath made (1864)
*Thou eternal life bestowest (1864)
*Thou hast borne our sins and sorrows (1875)
*Thou shalt rise! my dust thou shalt arise (1855)
*Thus said the Lord--thy days of health are over (1858)
*Times are changing, days are flying (1859)
*Voices of spring, with what gladness I hear you again (1862)

    *We praise and bless Thee, gracious Lord (1855)
    *What God does, that is rightly done (1864)
    *What no human eye hath seen (1855)
    *Whither, oh whither?--with blindfolded eyes (1858)
    *Yes! our Shepherd leads with gentle hand (1854)
    *Yes, still for us a rest remaineth (1869)

BOURDILLON, Mary Cotterill (1819-1870). British. Church of
    England

    A Mother's Hymns for Her Children (1849, 1852)

    Above the clear blue sky (1849)
    Blessed Jesus, wilt Thou hear us? (1849)
    Gracious Saviour, from on high (1849)
    Jesus, we thank Thee for Thy day (1849)
    Lamb of God, who came from heaven (1849)
    My God has given me work to do (1849)
    There was a lovely Garden once (1849)

BRAWN, Mary Ann (b. 1828). British. Baptist

    God of glory, at Thy feet (1867)
    O Father, we are very weak (1879)
    O Thou Who art in every place (1850)
    O'er life's tempestuous sea (1850)

BRONTË, Anne (1819-1849). British. Church of England

    I hoped that with the brave and strong (1846)
    My God, O let me call Thee mine (1846)
    Oppressed with sin and woe (1846)
    Spirit of truth, be Thou my guide (1846)

BROOK, Frances (b. 1870). British. Church of England

    My goal is God Himself (1896)
    My home is God Himself (1899)
    O Lord, with Thee 'tis but a little matter (1896)

BROTHERTON, Alice Williams. American

    Consider the lilies, how stately they grow (1905)

BROWN, Jeanette Eloise Perkins (1887-1960).   American

> *As Children Worship* (1936)
> *A Little Book of Singing Graces* (1946)
>
> Thanks be to God, for blessings (1946)
> We thank Thee, God, for eyes to see (1936)

BROWN, Leila Jackson (b. 1930)

> *Listen to our prayer (1956)

BROWN, Phoebe Hinsdale (1783-1861).   American.   Congregational

> As once the Savior took His seat (1824)
> Assembled at Thine altar, Lord (1836)
> Go, messenger of love, and bear (1817, 1824)
> Grant the abundance of the sea (1836)
> Great God, we would to Thee make known (1834)
> How sweet the melting lay (1819, 1831)
> I love to steal awhile away (1818, 1824)
> Jesus, this mid-day hour (1857)
> O Lord, Thy work revive (1819, 1831)
> We come, O Lord, before Thy throne (1836)
> Welcome, ye hopeful heirs of heaven (1824)

BROWNING, Elizabeth Barrett (1806-1861).   British.   Church of
      England

> God, named love, whose Fount Thou art
> How high Thou art! Our songs can own
> Of all the thoughts of God, that are
> When Jesus' friend had ceased to be
>
> (The above poems first appeared *as hymns* in 1853 and 1855.)

BUCHANAN, Violet Nita (b. 1891).   British.   Church of England

> O day of joy and wonder (1957, 1965)

BULMER, Agnes Collinson (1775-1837).   British.   Methodist

> Thou art in Zion laid (1825, 1830)

BURLINGHAM, Hannah Kilham (1842-1901).   British

> *A few short days of trial here (1865)

*Ah! Jesus! Lord! whose faithfulness (1867)
*Another year we now have enter'd (1866)
*As God doth lead me, will I go (1866)
*As truly as I live, God saith (1865)
*Brightness of external day (1866)
*Christ the Author of our peace (1866)
*Have thy armour on, my soul (1865)
*How beauteous shines the morning star (1865)
*Jerusalem! thou city builded high (1866)
*Jesus! Jesus! come to me (1865)
*Jesus! source of life eternal (1865)
*Looking from this vale of sadness (1865)
*Lord, none to Thee may be compared (1866)
*Love divine! my love commanding (1865)
*O anxious care that weighs me down (1865)
*O come, my soul, with singing (1866)
*O gentle Shepherd by Thy staff directed (1865)
*O Jesus, at Thy shining (1865)
*O Jesus, Friend unfailing (1865)
*O my heart, be calm, confiding (1866)
*O precious Jesus, what hast Thou been doing (1865)
*O tell me not of gold and treasure (1865)
*Prince of Peace! Thy name confessing (1866)
*Still on my native shore my feet are standing (1865)
*Thou, Jesu, art my consolation (1866)
*Thrice happy he who serveth (1865)
*'Tis spring, the time of singing (1866)
*To Thee, O Lord, I come with singing (1866)
*Up! Christian! gird thee to the strife (1865)
*With the glow of ardent longing (1865)
*Wrestle on! for God is pleading (1865)

BURMAN, Ellen Elizabeth (1837-1861). British

   Teach me to live! (1860, 1862)

BURROWES, Elisabeth (b. 1885)

   God of the ages by whose hand (1958)

BUTLER, Mary May (1841-1916). British. Church of England

   Looking upward every day (1881)
   O help me, Lord, this day to be (1881)
   Whiteness of the winter's snow (1905)

BYRNE, Mary Elizabeth (1880-1931). Irish

   *Be thou my vision, O Lord of my heart (1905)

CADDELL, Cecelia Mary (1813-1877). British. Roman Catholic

      A little boat, with snow-sail (1853)
      Behold the lilies of the field (1853)
      Dear Saint, who on thy natal day (1853)
      Hail! Mary, only sinless child (1853)
      It is finished! He hath seen (1853)
      Maiden Mother, meek and mild (1853)
      O Jesu, it were surely sweet (1853)

CAIN, Florence Emily. American. Methodist

      God of truth from everlasting (1970)

CAMPBELL, Etta. American

      Come, ye children, sweetly sing (1864)
      What means this eager, anxious throng (1863)

CAMPBELL, Jane Montgomery (1817-1878). British. Church of
      England

   *Holy night! peaceful night! all is dark (1863)
   *We plough the fields, and scatter (1861)

CARNEY, Julia A. Fletcher (b. 1823). American

      Little drops of water (1845)

CARPENTER, Mary (1807-1877). British. Unitarian

      Father, here Thy glory praising (1849)
      To Thee, my God, to Thee (1845)

CARR, Mrs. E.J.

   *Behold, a Lamb! so tired and faint (1871)

CARR, Johanna Stanley

   *All hail to Thee, my Saviour and my God (1856)

    *And oft I think, if e'en earth's sin-stained ground (1845)
    *Commit thy ways, thy sorrows (1845)
    *Full of wonder, full of skill (1856)
    *The world may fall beneath my feet (1845)

CARY, Alice (1820-1871). American. Universalist

    A crown of glory bright (1868)
    Along the mountain track of life (1855)
    Bow, angels, from your glorious state (1868)
    Earth, with its dark and dreadful ills (1870)
    I cannot plainly see the way (1868)
    Leave me, dear ones, to my slumber (1868)
    Light waits for us in heaven (1868)
    O day to sweet religious thought (1866)
    Our days are few and full of strife (1866)
    To Him Who is the Life of life (1866)

CARY, Phoebe (1824-1871). American. Universalist

    Hymns for All Christians, with Charles F. Deems (1869)

    Go and sow beside all waters (1868)
    Great waves of plenty rolling up (1868)
    I had drunk, with lips unsated (1868)
    One sweetly solemn thought (1852)

CHANT, Laura Ormiston Dibdin (b. 1848). British. Church of
    England

    Beyond the far horizon (1891)
    Light of the world, faint were our weary feet (1901, 1904)
    Silence, O earth, and listen to the song (n.d.)

CHARLES, Elizabeth Rundle (1828-1896). British. Church of
    England

    Three Wakings, with Hymns and Songs (1859)
    *The Voice of Christian Life in Song; or, Hymns and Hymn
      Writers of Many Lands and Ages* (1858)

    *A Lamb goes uncomplaining forth (1858)
    Age after age shall call Thee blessed (1859)
    *Ah! hush now your mournful complainings (1858)
    *All the world's salvation hail (1858)
    *Alleluia, sweetest music (1858)
    Around a table, not a tomb (1862, 1868)

   *At length the longed-for joy is given (1858)
   *Be not dismay'd, Thou little flock (1858)
   *Christ, Who art both our light and day (1858)
    Come and rejoice with me (1846, 1859)
   *Commit thy way to God (1858)
   *Dear Christian people, all rejoice (1858)
   *Hail, festal day, ever exalted (1858)
   *Hail, Thou Head! so bruised and wounded (1858)
    Is the cruse of comfort wasting (1859)
   *It is the midnight hour (1858)
   *Jesu, our Redeemer, now (1858)
   *Jesus, my eternal trust (1858)
    Jesus, what once Thou wast (1881)
   *Joyful light of holy glory (1858)
   *Lo the day of wrath, the day (1858)
   *Lo the day, the day of life (1858)
    Master, where abidest Thou? (1859)
    Never further than Thy Cross (1860)
    No Gospel like this Feast (1859)
   *O Christ! how good and fair (1858)
   *O God, my heart is fixed on Thee (1858)
   *Redeemer of the nations, come (1858)
   *Small amongst cities, Bethlehem (1858)
   *Suddenly to all appearing the great day of God shall come
      (1858)
   *The blessed Cross now to us where once the Saviour bled
      (1858)
   *The Child is born in Bethlehem (1858)
    The little birds fill all the air with their glee (1859)
   *The renewal of the world (1858)
   *Thou deep abyss of blessed love (1858)
   *Till the thirty years were finished (1867)
    Toss'd with rough winds, and faint with fear (1859)
    What marks the dawning of the year? (1859)
   *Yesterday the happy earth (1858)

CHESTER, Henrietta Mary Goff. British. Church of England

   *Come, let us all with one accord (1872)
    Holy Trinity, before Thee (n.d.)
   *In the far celestial land (1872)
   *Lo! the world from slumber risen (1872)
   *Praise to Thee, O Lord, most holy (1872)
   *The strains of joy that ceaseless flow (1872)
   *To Barnabas, Thy servant blest (1872)
   *Wake hearts devout whom love inspires (1872)
   *What God does is done aright (1872)

CLAPHAM, Emma (b. 1830).   British.   Congregational

>   Guide of my steps along life's way (1858)
>   Lord, we meet to pray and praise (1858)
>   Saviour, where dwellest Thou? (1858)

CLAPP, Eliza Thayer.   American

>   All before us lies the way (1841)

CLARE, Mary F. [Margaret Anna Cusack] (1829-1899).   Irish.
>   Roman Catholic

>   *Hymns for Children, by a Religious of the Holy Order of
>   the Poor Clares* (1862)

>   Before the throne of God above (1862)
>   Hark the angels bright are singing (1862)
>   Jesus was once a little child (1862)
>   O gentle Jesus, had I been (1862)
>   When Jesus was on earth He used (1862)

CLARK, Bertha L. (fl. 1901).   American

>   There is a noble river (1901)

CLARK, Emily V.

>   O God of mercy! hearken now (1891)

CLARKE, Sara Klein

>   Because God loves all people (1959)
>   For a winter world of white (1959)
>   Good news to tell (1959)
>   When Jesus taught the word of God (1961)

CLARKSON, Edith Margaret (b. 1915).   Canadian.   Presbyterian

>   For Thy gift, the God of Spirit (1964)
>   We come, O Christ, to Thee (1946, 1948)

CLEPHANE, Anna Jane Douglas Maclean (1793-1860).   Scottish.
>   Free Church of Scotland (Presbyterian)

>   Toiling in the path of duty (1882)

CLEPHANE, Elizabeth Cecelia Douglas (1830-1869).   Scottish.
        Free Church of Scotland (Presbyterian)

    Beneath the Cross of Jesus (1872)
    Dim eyes for ever closed (1872)
    From my dwelling midst the dead (1873)
    Into His summer garden (1873)
    Life-light waneth to an end (1874)
    The day is drawing nearly done (1873)
    There were ninety and nine that safely lay (1868)
    Who climbeth up too high (1872)

COBBE, Frances Power (1822-1904).   Irish.   United Church of
        England and Ireland

    God draws a cloud over each gleaming morn (1859)

COCKBURN-CAMPBELL, Lady Margaret Malcolm (1807-1841).   British.
        Plymouth Brethren

    Poor wanderer, return to the home of thy bliss (1839, 1842)
    Praise ye Jehovah, praise the Lord most holy (1838, 1842)
    Yet a little while (1830, 1831)

CODNER, Elizabeth Harris (b. 1835).   British.   Church of England

    Even me, even me (n.d.)
    Lord, I hear of showers of Blessing (1860)
    Lord, to Thee my heart ascending (1867)

COGHILL, Annie Louisa Walker (1836-1907).   British-Canadian
    Work for the night is coming (1854)

COLLIER, Mary Ann (1810-1866).   American.   Baptist
    The sun that lights yon broad blue sky (1843)

COLLINS, Mrs. S.A. (b. 1830).   American.   Baptist
    Jesus, gracious One, calleth now to thee (1881)

COLQUHOUN, Frances Sara Fuller-Maitland (1809-1877). British.
    Church of England

    Launched upon the stormy ocean (1827)
    There is a vale in Israel's road (1863)
    Will ye flee in danger's hour (1827)

CONDER, Joan Elizabeth Thomas (1785-1877). British. Congrega-
    tional

    Not Thy garment's hem alone (1836)
    The hours of evening close (1836)
    What blissful harmonies above (1836)
    When Mary to the Heavenly Guest (1836)

COOK, Eliza (1817-1899). British

    Father above, I pray to Thee (1860)

COOTE, Maude Oswell (1852-1935). British. Church of England

    The Son of consolation! of Levi's priestly line (1871)
    The strain of joy and gladness (1871)

COPENHAVER, Laura Scherer (1868-1940). American. United
    Lutheran

    Heralds of Christ, who bear the King's commands (n.d.)

CORELLI, Marie (1855-1924). British

    In our hearts celestial voices softly say (1901)

CORY, Julia Bulkley Cady (1882-1963). American. Presbyterian

    We praise Thee, O God our Redeemer, Creator (1902)

COTTERILL, Jane Boak (1790-1825). Scottish. Presbyterian

    O! from the world's vile slavery (1815)
    O Thou! Who has at Thy command (1815)

COUSIN, Anne Ross Cundell (1824-1906). Scottish. Free Church
    of Scotland (Presbyterian)

    King eternal, King immortal (1876)

None but Christ; His merit hides me (1876)
O! Christ He is the fountain (1857)
O Christ, what burdens bowed Thy head (1876)
Saviour, shed Thy sweetest blessing (1865)
The sands of time are sinking (1857)
To Thee, and to Thy Christ, O God (1876)
To thy father and thy mother (1876)
When we reach our peaceful dwelling (1876)

COWPER, Frances Maria Madan (1727–1797). British. Church of
    England

My span of life will soon be done (1792)

COX, Frances Elizabeth (1812–1897). British. Church of
    England

Hymns from the German (1841)
Sacred Hymns from the German (1841)

*A fortress firm and steadfast rock (1864)
*A holy, pure, and spotless lamb (1864)
*A new and contrite heart create (1841)
*A thousand years have fleeted (1841)
*Bear Jesus Christ the Lord in mind (1863)
*Come, enter Thine own portal (1864)
*Come forth, my heart, and seek delight (1841)
*Come, tune your heart (1841)
*Earth has nothing sweet or fair (1841)
*Encumber'd heart! lay by Thy sorrow (1841)
*Eternity! Eternity!--yet onward (1841)
*From blest, unconscious sleep I wake again (1864)
*Go! and let my grave be made (1841)
*Good and pleasant 'tis to see (1841)
*Heaven and earth and sea and air, God's eternal (1841)
*Heavenward still our pathway tends (1841)
*How lovely now the morning star (1864)
*I sing to Thee with mouth and heart (1864)
*Jerusalem! thou city towering high (1864)
*Jesus lives! no longer now (1864)
*Jesus, Lord, Thy servants see (1841)
*Life's course must recommence to-day (1841)
*Lo! God to Heaven ascendeth (1841)
*Lo! my choice is now decided (1841)
*Lo! now the victory's gain'd me (1841)
*Love, Who in the first beginning (1864)

*Mortals who have God offended (1841)
*Most high and holy Trinity, Thou God (1841)
*My restless heart, with anguish moaning (1841)
*My Saviour, make me cleave to Thee (1841)
*My soul! let this your thoughts employ (1841)
*Now hushed are woods and waters (1864)
*O fear not, Christians, that rough path to tread (1864)
*O God, whose attributes shine forth in turn (1864)
*O Holy Ghost! Thy heavenly dew (1841)
*O Lord! I long Thy face to see (1841)
*O! let him whose sorrow (1841)
*O ye your Saviour's name who bear (1841)
*Oh! what is human life below (1864)
*One thing's needful, then, Lord Jesus (1841)
*Raise high the notes of exultation (1841)
*Seven times our blessed Saviour spoke (1841)
*Sing praise to God who reigns above (1864)
*Soul! couldst Thou, while on earth remaining (1841)
*Steep and thorny is the way to our home (1841)
*Sunbeams all golden (1864)
*Sunk is the sun's last beam of light (1841)
*The day is o'er, my soul longs sore (1864)
*The last days will come indeed (1841)
*The mighty Saviour comes from heaven (1841)
*The wandering sages trace from far (1841)
*This day sent forth His heralds bold (1867)
*This holy feast, by Jesus spread (1863)
*Thou good and gracious God (1864)
*Wake! the startling watch-cry pealeth (1864)
*Wake! the welcome day appeareth (1841)
*We come, our hearts with gladness glowing (1841)
*We sing to Thee, Emmanuel, the Prince (1864)
*What God hath done is done aright (1864)
*What laws, my blessed Saviour, hast Thou broken (1864)
*When afflictions sore oppress you (1841)
*Who are these like stars appearing? (1841)
*Why is it that life is no longer sad? (1869)
*Wilt Thou not, my Shepherd true (1841)
*With sorrow now for past misdeeds (1864)
*With tears o'er lost Jerusalem (1841)
*Within a Garden's bound (1864)

CREWDSON, Jane Fox (1809-1863). British

    Give to the Lord Thy heart (1864)
    How tenderly Thy hand is laid (1864)
    I want a Sabbath talk with Thee (1864)

I've found a joy in sorrow (1864)
Looking unto Jesus (1864)
Lord, we know that Thou art near us (1864)
O for the peace which floweth as a river (1860)
O Saviour, I have nought to plead (1864)
O Thou whose bounty fills my cup (1860)
One touch from Thee, the Healer of diseases (1864)
The followers of the Son of God (1864)
There is no sorrow, Lord, too light (1860)
Though gloom may veil our troubled skies (1864)
'Tis not the Cross I have to bear (1864)

CROPPER, Margaret Beatrice (b. 1886). British

Jesu's hands were kind hands (1950)
Take our gifts, O loving Jesus (1950)

CROSS, Ada Cambridge (b. 1844). British. Church of England

Hymns on the Holy Communion (1866)
Hymns on the Litany (1865)

Humbly now with deep contrition (1865)
Jesus, great Redeemer (1866)
Light of the world, O shine on us (1865)
Saviour, by Thy sweet compassion (1865)
The dawn of God's dear Sabbath (1866)

CROZIER, Maria P. Alger. American

Home at last on heavenly mountains (1878)
Only a little while (n.d.)

CUNNINGGIM, Maude Merrimon (1874-1965)

O living Christ, chief cornerstone (1935)

DANA, Mary Stanley Bounce Palmer Shindler (b. 1810). American.
    Presbyterian, Unitarian, Protestant Episcopal

Fiercely came the tempest sweeping (1841)
Flee as a bird to your mountain (1841)
I'm a pilgrim, and I'm a stranger (1841)
O sing to me of heaven (1840)
Once upon the heaving ocean (n.d.)
Prince of Peace, control my will (1858)

DAYE, Elizabeth (1733-1829). British. Unitarian

I'll bless Jehovah's glorious name (1795)
O may the truths this day has taught (n.d.)

DECK, Mary Ann Sanderson Gibson (1813-1902). British

There is a city bright (1898)

DeFLEURY, Maria (d. 1794). British. Baptist

O garden of Olivet, dear honour'd spot (1791)
Thou soft flowing Kedron, by thy silver stream (1791)
Ye angels who stand round the throne (1791)

DEMAREST, Mary Lee (1838-1887). American

I am frae from home (1861)

DEMING, Mary W.

Come softly, walk gently to see what is there (1937)

DENT, Caroline (1815-1901). British. Baptist

Jesus Saviour! Thou dost know (n.d.)
The light that morning bringeth (1900)

DOBREE, Henrietta Octavia DeLisle (1831-1894). British. Church
    of England, Roman Catholic

Again the morning shines so bright (1881)
Lord, we come to ask Thy blessing (1881)
O my God, I fear Thee (1881)
Our solemn Lent has come again (1881)
Safely, safely gathered in (1881)

DOUDNEY, Sarah (1843-1926). British

For all Thy care we bless (1871)
In Thy holy garden ground (1871)
Land of peace, and love, and brightness (1871)
Lord of the golden harvest (1871)
Now the solemn shadows darken (1881)
Saviour, now the day is ending (1871)

The Master hath come, and He tells us to follow (1871)
We praise our Lord to-day (1871)
We sing a loving Jesus (1871)

DOUGHFMAN, Betty

A little boy in Galilee (1959)
Dear Father, hear my prayer to Thee (1959)
The Bible tells of God's great love (1959)

DRANE, Augusta Theodosia (1823-1894). British. Roman Catholic

O spouse of Christ, on whom (1881)
The clouds hang thick o'er Israel's camp (1885)
Thou who hero-like hast striven (1862)

DRURY, Miriam. American

Give us a dream to share (1970)
Once again to its close (n.d.)
This is our prayer, dear God (1942)
Within the Church's hallowed walls (1969)

DUCKERT, Mary

I am learning to read the Bible (1960)
We gather here to sing to God (1960)
When we hear Scripture read in church (1960)

DUNCAN, Mary Lundie (1814-1840). Scottish. Presbyterian

Jesus, tender Shepherd, hear me (1839, 1841)
My Saviour, be Thou near me (1839, 1841)

DUNN, Catherine Hannah (1815-1863). British

Hymns from the German (1857)

*Children rejoice, for God is come to earth (1857)
*Come, O Thou holy dove (1857)
*Dear Saviour, for me hast borne (1857)
*Draw us, Saviour, then will we (1857)
*Flowers that in Jesu's garden have a place (1853)
*God is our rock and tower of strength (1857)
*Heavenward our pathway lies (1857)
*Help, Lord Jesus, let Thy blessing (1857)

*In the grey of the morning when shades pass away (1857)
*It is finished! finished! yea (1857)
*Jesus is the sinner's friend (1857)
*Jesus, Saviour, once again (1857)
*Jesus, 'tis my aim divine (1857)
*My Shepherd is the Saviour dear (1857)
*O gentle Shepherd, guided by Thy hand (1853)
*O Head, blood-stained and wounded (1857)
*O Thou blessed light of light (1857)
*One, only one, shall be the fold (1857)
*Rise, my soul, thy vigil keep (1857)
*See, bowed beneath a fearful weight (1857)
*The Lord is here; then let us bow before him (1857)
*The shades of night have banished day (1857)
*The sun's golden beams (1857)
*Thou holiest Saviour, sacred spring (1857)
*Treasure beyond all treasure (1857)
*Upwards, upwards to Thy gladness (1857)
*What pleaseth God with joy receive (1857)
*When, only dearest Lord, I prove (1857)
*While on earth, dear Lord, I roam (1857)
*Whither shall we flee (1857)
*Why this sad and mournful guise (1857)
*World farewell, my soul is weary (1857)

DUNSTERVILLE, Patty Caroline Sellon (1831-1877).   British.
    Church of England

    The day is done:--O God the Son (1882)

DURAND, Lady Emily Allnat Polehampton.   British.   Church of
    England

    *A rough and shapeless block of iron is my heart (1873)
    *Ah, could I but be still (1873)
    *Fountain of all salvation, we adore Thee (1873)
    *From all created things (1873)
    *God, in whom I have my being (1873)
    *I know Thy voice, my Shepherd (1873)
    *Jesus, my Sun, before whose beams (1873)
    *Jesus, with Thee I would abide (1873)
    *Jesus, whom I long for (1873)
    *My heart is bright with joy (1873)
    *O blessed are ye messengers, sent forth (1873)
    *O how many an hour of gladness (1873)
    *O will of God, all sweet and perfect (1873)
    *One more flying moment (1873)

    *Return, return, Thou lost one (1873)
    *Sleep not, O soul by God awakened (1873)
    *The outer sunlight now is there (1873)
    *Thus, step by step, my journey to the Infinite (1873)
    *Thus, then another year of pilgrim-life (1873)
    *Weary heart, be not desponding (1873)
    *With brighter glory, Easter sun (1873)

DUTTON, Anne (1698-1765). British. Baptist

    Faith is a precious grace (1734, 1833)
    The soul's joy in God as its portion (1734, 1833)

EDDY, Mary Baker Glover (1821-1910). American. Christian
    Science

    Blest Christmas morn (n.d.)
    Brood o'er us with Thy sheltering (n.d.)
    It matters not what be Thy lot (n.d.)
    O gentle presence, peace (n.d.)
    O'er waiting harp-strings (n.d.)
    Saw ye my Saviour? (n.d.)
    Shepherd, show me how to go (n.d.)

EDGAR, Mary S. (b. 1889)

    God, who touchest earth with beauty (1925)
    I will follow the upward road (n.d.)

EDWARDS, Annie (b. 1832). British. Moravian

    He must reign who won the right (1881)

EDWARDS, Matilda Barbara Betham (1836-1919). British

    God, make my life a little light (1873)
    The little birds now seek their rest (1873)

ELLIOTT, Charlotte (1789-1871). British. Church of England

    Hymns for a Week (1839)
    The Invalid's Hymn Book (1834, 1841, 1854)

    Another portion of the span (1839)
    Art thou acquainted, O my soul? (1834)

As the new moons of old were given (1869)
Christian, seek not repose (1839)
Clouds and darkness round about Thee (1841)
Ever patient, gentle, meek (1834)
Father, when thy child is dying (1835)
Glorious was that primal light (1835)
God of my life, Thy boundless grace (1841)
Guard well thy lips; none can know (1839)
Hail, holy day, most blest, most dear (1836)
I need no other plea (1869)
I need no prayers to saints (1869)
I want that adorning divine (1848)
Immortal Spirit! wake, arise (1839)
Jesus, my Saviour, look on me (1869)
Just as I am, without one plea (1836)
Leaning on Thee, my Guide, my Friend (1836)
Let me be with Thee where Thou art (1836)
My God and Father! while I stray (1834)
My God, is any hour so sweet? (1836)
My only Saviour, when I feel (1835)
Not willingly dost Thou afflict (1841)
Now let our heavenly plants and flowers (1838)
Now one day's journey less divides (1836)
O faint and feeble-hearted (1836)
O God, may I look up to Thee (1841)
O Jesus, make Thyself to me (1862, 1872)
O Thou, the contrite sinner's friend (1835)
The dawn approaches, golden streaks (1869)
The Sabbath day has reached its close (1835)
There is a holy sacrifice (1819)
There is a spot of consecrated (1839)
This is enough; although 'twere sweet (1834)
This is the day to tune with care (1839)
This is the moment where Christ's disciples see (1839)
Thou glorious Sun of righteousness (1839)
When waves of trouble round me swell (1834)
With tearful eyes I look around (1835)

ELLIOTT, Emily Elizabeth Steele (1836-1897). British. Church
    of England

    Brothers, sisters, pray for us (1896)
    Full consecration! heart and spirit yielded (1902)
    Have you ever brought a penny to the missionary box? (1855)
    Rabboni, Master, we have heard (1895)
    Sowers went throughout the land (1872)
    *Stilly night, Holy night, silent stars (1858, 1871)

There came a little child to earth (1856)
They come and go, the seasons fair (1891)
Thou didst leave Thy throne and Thy kingly crown (1864)
Unto Him whose name is holy (1866)

ELLIOTT, Julia Ann Marshall (1809-1841). British. Church of
    England

Father, if that gracious name (1835)
Great Creator, who this day (1835)
Hail, thou bright and sacred morn (1835)
I would believe; but my weak heart (1835)
My God, and can I linger still (1835)
O not when o'er the trembling soul (1835)
O Thou, who didst this rite reveal (1835)
On the dewy breath of even (1835)
Soon, too soon, the sweet repose (1835)
We love Thee, Lord, yet not alone (1835)
Welcome to me, the darkest night (1835)

ESLING, Catherine H. Watterman (1812-1897). American. Protes-
    tant Episcopal

Come unto me, when shadows darkly gather (1839)

FAGAN, Frances. American. Unitarian

Mine be the tongue that always shrinks (1875)
The still small voice that speaks within (1875)

FARJEON, Eleanor (b. 1881)

Morning has broken like the first morn (1931)

FAUSSETT, Alessie Bond (b. 1841). Irish. United Church of
    England and Ireland

Be with us all for ever more (1867)
O Lamb of God that tak'st away (1865)

FELKIN, Ellen Thorneycroft Fowler. British. Methodist

Now the year is crowned with blessing (1904)

FERGUSON, Jessie Margaret MacDougall (1895-1964). Scottish.
    United Free Church (Presbyterian)

    Gentle Jesus, hear our prayer (1937)
    We thank Thee, Lord, for all Thy gifts (1935)

FINDLATER, Sarah Laurie Borthwick (1823-1907). Scottish. Free
    Church of Scotland (Presbyterian)

    Hymns from the Land of Luther (see Borthwick, Jane Laurie)

    *Ah, Christian! if the needy poor (1858)
    *Ah! grieve not so, nor so lament (1854)
    *Ah! the heart that has forsaken (1859)
    *Be Thou my friend, and look upon my heart (1858)
    *Behold me here, in grief draw near (1854)
    *Christ's path was sad and lowly (1858)
    *Come brothers, let us onward (1854)
    *Flow my tears, flow still faster (1855)
    *God calling yet!--and shall I never harken? (1855)
    *Give us Thy blessed peace, God of all might (1862)
    *Here am I, Lord, Thou callest me (1862)
    *Here is my heart! my God I give it Thee (1854)
    *I have had my days of blessing (1855)
    *I know a sweet and silent spot (1858)
    *I will love Thee, all my Treasure (1855)
    *Jesus! what was that which drew Thee (1855)
    *Lord our God, in reverence lowly (1858)
    *Loved one! who by grace hast wrought me (1862)
    *My father is the mighty Lord (1854)
    *My God! I know that I must die (1854)
    *My God with me in every place (1854)
    *My heart wakes with a joyful lay (1862)
    *Oh! sweetest words that Jesus could have sought (1855)
    *Our beloved have departed (1855)
    *Rejoice, all ye believers (1854)
    *The Cross is ever good (1862)
     The Father knows thee! learn of Him (1862)
    *The Lord shall come in dread of night (1858)
    *This life is like a flying dream (1858)
    *We are the Lord's!--in life, in death remaining (1862)
    *Weary, waiting to depart (1855)
    *Weep not,--Jesus lives on high (1854)
    *What God decrees, child of His love (1858)
    *What shall I be? my Lord, when I behold Thee (1855)
    *Where the lambs sleep, there shepherds watch around (1862)
    *Will that not joyful be? (1854)
    *Yes! it shall be well at morning (1862)

FLOWERDEW, Alice (1759-1830). British. Baptist

    Fountain of mercy, God of love (1803)

FOLLEN, Elizabeth Cabot (1787-1860). American. Unitarian

    Go forth, my heart, and seek the bliss (1854)
    God, Thou art good, each perfumed flower (1825)
    How sweet to be allowed to pray (1818)
    How sweet upon this sacred day (1829)
    Lord, deliver, Thou canst save (1836)
    Will God who made the earth and sea (1839)

FORSYTH, Christina (1825-1859). British. Church of England

    Hymns by C.F. (1861)

    Himself hath done it all (1861)
    Jehovah elohim! Creator great (1861)
    O Holy Spirit, now descend on me (1861)
    O what a happy lot is mine (1861)

FORTESQUE, Lady Eleanor (1798-1874). British. Church of
    England

    Hymns Mostly Taken from the German (1843, 1847, 1849)

    *At eve appears the Morning star (1843)
    *Awake! awake! from careless ease (1843)
    *Behold how sweet it is to see (1843)
    *Blest Spirit, by whose heavenly dew (1843)
    *From Heaven comes the mighty Lord (1843)
    *Go forth, Thou mighty words of grace (1843)
    *Heaven and ocean, earth and air (1843)
    *Heavenward may our course begin (1843)
    *I now commence a separate stage (1843)
    *Jesus! I place my trust in Thee (1843)
    *Lift up my soul to Thee, O Lord (1843)
    *Lo! steep and thorny is the road (1843)
    *Lord! grant a new-born heart to me (1843)
    *Most holy God! to Thee I cry (1843)
    *My God! when will Thy heavenly peace (1843)
    *My Saviour lives! I will rejoice (1843)
    *My soul is thirsting, Lord, for Thee (1843)
    *Now weary heart! thy care dismiss (1843)
    *O Blessed Saviour! here we meet (1843)
    *O Faithful Shepherd! now behold (1843)
    *O Lord, Thy goodness we adore (1843)

*O ye who bear your Saviour's name (1843)
*Prepare me now my narrow bed (1843)
*Sweet slumbers now thine eyelids close (1843)
*The sun hath run his daily race (1843)
*Think, O my soul, that whilst thou art (1843)
*Thy mercy, Lord, is still the same (1843)
*When affliction rends the heart (1843)
*When in thine hours of grief (1843)
*Whate'er of beauty I behold (1843)
*Wouldst thou, my soul, the secret find (1843)

FOX, Eleanor Frances (b. 1875). British. Church of England

God of all pity and all power (1899)
I know that Jesus died for me (1899)
Saviour, to Whom the sound of sorrows sighing (1899)

FREER, Frances (1801-1901). British. Catholic and Apostolic
    Church

Present the two or three (1871)

FRITZ, Dorothy B.

For all Thy gifts of love our thanks we give (1949)
God's people all around the world (1959)
Wherever people live in love (1959)

FRY, Henrietta J. British

Hymns of the Reformation (1845)

*Almighty God, Thy truth shall stand (1845)
*Around me all is joy--and oh, my God (1859)
*Awake! awake! the watchman calls (1845)
*Behold that bright, that hallowed ray (1845)
*Behold the Father's love (1859)
*Behold! Thy goodness, oh my God (1845)
*Clothe me, oh Lord, with strength (1859)
*Come, thou creator God (1845)
*Eternity! that word, that joyful word (1845)
*From yon ethereal heavens (1845)
*God is the city of our strength (1845)
*Holy Spirit, gracious Lord (1845)
*How long, O God, Thy word of life (1845)
*I come, I come! from yon celestial clime (1845)
*If God were not upon our side (1845)
*Jesus, my Sun! before whose eye (1859)

*Lo! in the East the golden morn appearing (1859)
*Lord, in Thy mercy and Thy grace (1845)
*Now may our God, His mercy (1845)
*Now the Saviour of the heathen (1845)
*O day! that hast unto our souls set forth (1859)
*O God! uphold us by Thy word (1845)
*O Lord our God! to Thee we raise, One universal (1845)
*Oh! could my soul possess His love (1845)
*Oh, let Thy praise, Redeemer, God! (1845)
*Oh Lord our God, from heaven look down (1845)
*Oh Lord! Thy presence through the day's distractions (1859)
*Once in the bands of death the Saviour lay (1845)
*Our Father in the heavenly realm (1845)
*Rise again! yes, Thou shalt rise again, my dust (1859)
*See! Triumphant over death (1845)
*Since Thou, the living God, art Three (1845)
*Soon shall that voice resound (1845)
*Surely none like Thee can teach (1845)
*To God alone in the highest heaven (1845)
*To Thee, Thou Holy Spirit, now (1845)
*We are the Lord's in living or in dying (1859)
*We read that to Isaiah it befel (1845)
*When we walk the paths of life (1845)
*With peace and joy from earth I go (1845)
*Ye messengers of Christ (1859)

FULLERTON, Lady Georgiana Charlotte (1812-1885). British.
     Roman Catholic

   Christ's soldier, rise (1860)
   I'll never forsake Thee (1860)
   In breathless silence kneel (1860)
   Mary, mother! shield us (1860)
   O heart of Jesus, heart of God (1872)

GARNIER, Emily. British. Church of England

   Think on the mercy of our God (1834, 1841)

GARRIOTT, Jean E. American. Disciples of Christ

   God of all nations, help us now (1975)
   World around us, sky above us (1970)

GATES, Ellen Huntington (1835-1920). American

> Come home, come home, you are weary of heart (n.d.)
> I will sing you a song of that beautiful land (n.d.)
> If you cannot on the ocean (1860)
> O the clanging bells of time (n.d.)
> Say, is your lamp burning, my brother (n.d.)

GATES, Mary Cornelia Bishop (1842-1905). American. Reformed
> Church

> Send Thou, O Lord, to every place (1890)

GILBERT, Ann Taylor (1782-1866). British. Congregational

> *Hymns for Infant Minds*, with Jane Taylor (1809, 1810; 35th
>   ed., 1844; 52nd ed., 1877)
> *Hymns for Infant Schools* (1827)
> *Hymns for Sunday School Anniversaries* (1827)
> *Hymns for the Nursery*, with Jane Taylor (1806)
> *Original Hymns for Sunday Schools*, with Jane Taylor (1812)

> Among the deepest shades of night (1810)
> And are there countries far away (1844)
> As Mary sat at Jesus' feet (1809)
> Father, my spirit owns (1842)
> God is in heaven! can He hear? (n.d.)
> Good Daniel would not cease to pray (1812)
> Great God, and wilt Thou condescend? (1810)
> Hark the sound of joy and gladness (1842)
> How long sometimes a day appears (1809)
> I faint, my soul doth faint (1842)
> I thank the goodness and the grace (1809)
> Jesus, that condescending King (1809)
> Jesus was once despised and low (1809)
> Jesus, Who lived above the sky (1812)
> Lo, at noon, 'tis sudden night (1810)
> Lord, help us as we hear (n.d.)
> Lord, what is life? 'tis like a flower (1809)
> My Father, I thank Thee for sleep (1809)
> O happy they who safely housed (1842)
> Spared to another spring (1827)
> The God of heaven is pleased to see (1809)
> This year is just going away (1810)
> Thou who didst for Peter's faith (1812)
> Unwearied with earthly toil and care (1843)
> When I listen to Thy word (n.d.)
> When little Samuel woke (1809)
> Why should we weep for those who die (1843)

Ellen Huntington Gates. From Tharon Brown and Hezekiah Butterworth. *The Story of the Hymns and Tunes.* New York: American Tract Society, 1906, p. 254.

GILBERT, Rosa Mulholland (d. 1921). Irish

    Give me, O Lord, a heart of grace (1905)

GILL, Sidney P. American

    I want to be an angel (1854)

GILMAN, Caroline Howard (1794-1888). American. Unitarian

    Is there a lone and dreary hour? (1820)
    We bless Thee for this sacred day (1820)

GLYDE, Elizabeth (1815-1845). British. Independent

    Be with me in the valley (1840, 1844)

GODWIN, Elizabeth Ayton Etheridge (1817-1889). British

    Songs amidst Daily Life (n.d.)
    Songs for the Weary (1865)

    My Saviour, 'mid life's varied scene (1873)

GOULD, Hannah Flagg (1789-1865). American

    Alone I walked the ocean strand (1832)
    Day of God, thou blessed day (1841)
    O Father, to the fields that are ripe (1832)
    O Thou who hast spread out the skies (1832)
    Who, when darkness gathered o'er us (1832)

GRAY, Jane Lewers (1796-1871). Irish-American. Presbyterian

    Am I called? and can it be (1834)
    Hark to the solemn bell (1842)

GREENAWAY, Ada Rundall (1861-1937). British. Church of England

    At the font, O loving Saviour (1897)
    For the dear ones parted from us (1904)
    Hear an echo of the message (1897)
    Hear the angels telling (1897)
    Hymns of thankfulness we raise (1897)
    Jesu, by the Lenten fast (1897)
    Lord, a little band of children (1897)

O Father, we would thank Thee (1904)
O perfect God, Thy love (1902, 1904)
O word of pity, for our pardon pleading (1904)
Saviour, hear us, as we plead (1897)

GREENSTREET, Annie Louise Ashley (b. 1835).   British

A little talk with Jesus (1871)

GREENWELL, Dorothy ("Dora") (1821-1882).   British.   Church of
England

Songs of Salvation (1872)
Two Friends: Songs of Salvation (1874)

I am not skilled to understand (1873)

GRIFFITHS, Ann (1776-1805).   Welsh

Hymnau ofawl i Dduw ar Oen [Hymns of Praise to God and the
Lamb] (pub. 1806, 1808)

GUINEY, Louise Imogen (1861-1920).   American.   Roman Catholic

The little cares that fretted (n.d.)

GURNEY, Dorothy Frances Bloomfield (1858-1932).   British.
Church of England

O perfect love, all human thought transcending (1883, 1889)

HALE, Mary Whitewell (1810-1862).   American.   Unitarian

Praise for the glorious light (1844)
This day let grateful praise ascend (1840)
Whatever dims the sense of truth (1840)
When in silence o'er the deep (1844)

HALE, Sarah Josepha Buell (1795-1879).   American.   Protestant
Episcopal

Our Father in heaven, we hallow Thy name (1831)

HALL, Elvina Mable (1818-1889). American. Methodist Episcopal

    I hear the Saviour say (1865)

HALL, Jane E. American

    The love that Jesus had for me (1881)
    We shall have a new name in that land (1881)

HAMILTON, Mary C.D. (b. 1915)

    Lord, guard and guide the men who fly (1934)

HANAFORD, Phoebe A. Coffin (b. 1829). American. Universalist

    Cast thy bread upon the waters (1884)

HANKEY, Arabella Katherine (1834-1911). British. Anglican
    Evangelical ("Clapham Sect")

    Advent tells us Christ is near (1870)
    I love to tell the story, of unseen things above (1868,
      1874)
    I saw Him leave His Father's throne (1868, 1879)
    Tell me the old, old story (1866)

HARDCASTLE, Carrie Hitt (b. 1894). American. Methodist

    Dear God of all creation (1975)
    O God, Thy Church eternal (1969)

HARKNESS, Georgia Elma (1891-1974). American. Methodist

    God of the fertile fields (1955)
    Hope of the world (1954)
    Shed Thou, O Lord, Thy light (1945)
    Tell it out with gladness (1966)
    The earth Thou gavest, Lord, is Thine (1961)

HARRISON, Susanna (1752-1784). British. Congregational

    Songs in the Night (1780)

    Begone, my worldly cares, away (1780)
    O happy souls that love the Lord (1780)

HASLOCH, Mary (1816-1892). British. Congregational

    Christian, work for Jesus (1887)

HASTINGS, Lady Flora (1806-1839). Scottish. Church of England

    O Thou, Who are for our fallen race (pub. 1841)

HAVERGAL, Frances Ridley (1836-1879). British. Church of
    England

   Ministry of Song (1869)
   Twelve Sacred Songs for Little Singers (1870)

   A happy new year! even such may it be (1874)
   Accepted, perfect, and complete (1870, 1871)
   Another called, another brought (1872)
   Another year is dawning (1874, 1875)
   As thy day thy strength shall be (1859, 1867)
   Begin at once! in the pleasant days (1876)
   Certainly I will be with Thee (1871)
   Church of God, beloved and chosen (1873)
   From glory unto glory (1873, 1874)
   God almighty, King of nations (1872)
   God doth not bid thee wait (1868)
   God of heaven, hear our saying (1869)
   God will take care of you, all through the day (1881)
   God's reiterated all (1873)
   Have you not a word for Jesus? (1871, 1872)
   He hath spoken in the darkness (1869, 1870)
   Hear the Father's ancient promise (1870, 1874)
   Holy and Infinite! viewless, eternal (1872, 1874)
   Holy brethren, called and chosen (1872)
   I am trusting Thee, Lord Jesus (1874)
   I bring my sins to Thee (1870)
   I could not do without Thee (1873)
   I give my life for Thee (1858, 1859)
   I love, I love my Master (1876, 1878)
   I love to feel that I am taught (1867, 1869)
   In full and glad surrender (1879)
   In God's great field of labour (1867, 1869)
   In the evening there is weeping (1869, 1870)
   Increase our faith, beloved Lord (1878)
   Is it for me, dear Saviour? (1871, 1872)
   Israel of God, awaken (1871, 1872)
   Jehovah's covenant shall endure (1872, 1876)
   Jesus, blessed Saviour (1872, 1873)
   Jesus, Master, whose I am (1865, 1869)

Jesus only! in the shadow (1870, 1871)
Jesus, Thy life is mine (1876)
Joined to Christ by mystic union (1871, 1872)
Just when Thou wilt, O Master, call (1878)
King eternal and immortal (1871, 1874)
Light after darkness, gain after loss (1879)
Like a river glorious, is God's perfect peace (1879)
Looking unto Jesus, never need we yield (1876)
Master, how shall I bless Thy name? (1875)
Master, speak! Thy servant heareth (1867, 1869)
New mercies, new blessings, new light on Thy way (1874)
Not your own, but His ye are (1867, 1869)
Now let us sing the angels' song (1879)
Now the daylight goes away (1869, 1870)
Now the sowing and the weeping (1870)
O, glorious God and King (1872, 1874)
O Master, at Thy feet (1866, 1867)
O Saviour, precious Saviour (1870)
O Thou chosen Church of Jesus (1871, 1874)
O what everlasting blessings God outpoureth on His own
    (1871)
Our Father, our Father, Who dwellest in light (1872, 1874)
Our Saviour and our King (1871)
Precious, precious blood of Jesus (1874)
Sing, O heavens, the Lord hath done it (1879)
Singing for Jesus, our Saviour and King (1872, 1874)
Sit down beneath His shadow (1870)
Sovereign Lord and gracious Master (1871, 1872)
Standing at the portal of the opening year (1873, 1874)
Take my life, and let it be (1874, 1878)
Tell it out among the heathen that the Lord is King (1872)
Thou art coming, O my Saviour (1873)
Through the yesterday of ages (1876, 1878)
To Thee, O Comforter divine (1872, 1874)
True-hearted, whole-hearted, faithful and loyal (1878)
Unfurl the Christian standard with firm and fearless hand
    (1872, 1874)
Unto him that hath Thou givest (1876)
What hast Thou done for me (1877, 1878)
What know we, Holy God, of Thee? (1872)
Who is on the Lord's side? (1877, 1879)
With quivering heart and trembling will (1866)
Will ye not come to Him for life? (1873)
Worthy of all adoration (1867, 1869)
Ye who hear the blessed call (1869)
Yes, He knows the way is dreary (1865, 1867)

HAWKINS, Hester Perriam (1846-1926). British

> *The Home and Empire Hymn Book* (n.d.)
> *The Home Hymn Book. A Manual of Sacred Song for the Family*
>   *Circle* (1885)

> Father of all, again we meet (1885)
> Heavenly Father, Thou hast brought us (1885)
> I come to Thee, my Father (1885)
> In the name of God our Father (1885)
> Jesu, loving Saviour (1885)
> Kind Shepherd, see Thy little lamb (1885)
> Now the days are dark and dreary (1885)
> O Thou the great unknown, unseen (1885)
> Sweetly o'er the meadows fair (1885)
> The happy days have come again (1885)
> The twilight softly falling (1885)
> There is a bright and happy home (1885)
> Thy little one, O Saviour dear (1885)
> To Thee, the giver of all good (1885)

HAWKS, Annie Sherwood (1835-1918). American. Baptist

> I need Thee every hour (1872)
> Thine, most gracious Lord (n.d.)
> Why weepest Thou? (n.d.)

HAYCRAFT, Margaret Scott MacRitchie. British. Church of
       England

> Bless the Lord forever (1896)
> Green the hills and lovely (1904, 1905)
> In golden light of early days (1906)
> Let there be light at eventide (1896)
> Thou art my Shepherd (1866)

HEAD, Bessie Porter (1850-1936). British

> O breath of life, come sweeping through us (1914)

HEADLAM, Margaret Ann (b. 1817). British. Church of England

> Holy is the seed-time when the buried grain (1862)
> Thy courts, O Lord, are open (1883)

HEARN, Marianne ["Marianne Farningham"] (1834-1909). British.
    Baptist

Morning and Evening Hymns for the Week (1870)
Songs of Sunshine (1878)

Anywhere with Jesus (1860)
Christ, we children sing to Thee (1881)
Father! abide with us (1860)
Father, who givest us now the new year (1878)
Hail the children's festal day (1875)
He smiled as He stretched out His hand (1906)
Just as I am, Thine own to be (1887)
Let the children come, Christ said (1877, 1881)
Little feet are passing (1866)
Sing, for the world rejoiceth (1887)
When mysterious whispers are floating about (1864)

HEATH, Eliza (1829-1905). British. Catholic Apostolic

Praise the Lord, sing Hallelujah (1864)

HEMANS, Felicia Dorothea Browne (1793-1835). British. Church
    of England

Hymns for Children (1827, 1834)
Scenes and Hymns of Life (1834)

Answer me, burning stars of light (1828)
Calm on the bosom of thy God (1823)
Child, amidst the flowers at play (1828)
Come to me, dreams of heaven (1834)
Come to the land of peace (1839)
Earth! guard what here we lay in holy trust (1839)
Father! that in the olive shade (1827)
Father! Who art on high (1834)
Fear was within the tossing bark (1827)
He knelt, the Saviour knelt and prayed (1825)
I hear Thee speak of the better land (1827)
Leaves have their time to fall (1827)
Lowly and solemn be Thy children's cry to Thee (1832)
No cloud obscures the summer's sky (1827)
Now autumn strews on every plain (1808)
O lovely voices of the sky (1827)
Praise ye the Lord on every height (1827)
Saviour, now receive him (1834)
The breaking waves dashed high (1828)
The Church of our fathers so dear to our souls (1834)

The kings of old have shrine and tomb (1829)
Where is the tree the prophet threw (1828)

HERNAMAN, Claudia Frances Ibotson (1838-1898). British.
    Church of England

*The Child's Book of Praise: A Manual of Devotion in Simple
    Verse* (1873)
Christmas Carols for Children (1884, 1885)
Hymns for the Seven Words from the Cross (1885)

Angels singing, church bells ringing (1875)
Arm, arm, for the conflict, soldiers (1880)
As Saint Joseph lay asleep (1878)
Behold, behold He cometh (1873)
Calling, calling, ever calling (1878)
Come, children, lift your voices (1878)
Early with the blush of dawn (1879)
Faithful Shepherd, hear our cry (1878)
Faithful Shepherd, of Thine own (1878)
God bless the Church of England (1878)
Gracious Father, we beseech Thee (1884)
Hail to Thee, O Jesu (1884)
Happy, happy Sunday (1878)
He led them unto Bethany (1878)
Holy Jesus, we adore Thee (1873)
Hosannah, they were crying (1873)
How can we serve Thee, Lord (1873)
It is a day of gladness (1881)
Jesu, we adore Thee (1878)
Jesus, in loving worship (1873)
Jesus, royal Jesus (1873)
Lord, I have sinned, but pardon me (1873)
Lord, who throughout these forty days (1873)
Magnify the Lord to-day (1884)
Now the six days' work is done (1879)
O Lamb of God, who dost abide (1884)
Reverently, we worship Thee (1873)
Shepherd, who Thy life didst give (1878)
This healthful mystery (1884)

HERSCHELL, Esther Fuller-Maitland (1803-1882). British. Church
    of England

Shrouded once in blackest night (1827)
Whence these sorrows, Saviour, say? (1827)

HEWITT, Eliza E.   (1851–1920)

   More about Jesus would I know (1887)

HINKSON, Katharine Tynan (1859–1931).   Irish.   Roman Catholic

   I would choose to be a door-keeper (n.d.)

HINSDALE, Grace Webster Haddock (1833–1902).   American.
      Congregational

   A light streams downward from the sky (1865)
   Are there no wounds for me? (1868, 1869)
   Jesus, the rays divine (1868, 1869)
   My soul complete in Jesus stands (1855, 1865)
   There was no angel 'midst the throng (1868, 1869)
   Thou stand'st between the earth and heaven (1867, 1869)

HORNBLOWER, Jane Roscoe (1797–1853).   British.   Unitarian

   How rich the blessings, O my God (1818)
   My Father, when around me spread (1828)
   O God, to Thee, Who first hast given (1820)
   Thy will be done, I will not fear (1843)

HOWE, Julia Ward (1819–1910).   American.   Unitarian

   Mine eyes have seen the glory of the coming of the Lord (186
      1862)

HOWITT, Mary Botham (1804–1888).   British.   Quaker

   Clothe me with Thy saving grace (1867)
   God might have made the earth bring forth (1837)
   How goodly is the earth (1839)
   Let me suffer, let me drain (1867)
   O spirit, freed from earth (1834)

HUEY, Mary Elizabeth (b. 1916).   American.   Presbyterian

   Serve the Lord with joy and gladness (1959)

HULL, Amelia Matilda (1825–1882).   British

   Heart Melodies (1864)
   A Hymn-Book for Children (n.d.)

Hymns by A.M.H. (1850)
The Silver Trumpet Answered (n.d.)

And is it true, as I am told? (1860)
There is life for a look at the crucified One (1860)

HULL, Eleanor Henrietta (1860-1935). Irish

   *Be Thou my vision, O Lord of my heart (1912)

HUMPHREYS, Jennett (b. 1829). British. Church of England

   March, my little children (1885)

HYDE, Abby Bradley (1799-1872). American. Congregational

   Ah, what can I a sinner do? (1824)
   And canst thou, sinner, slight? (1824)
   Behold the glorious dawning bright (1824)
   Dear Saviour, if these lambs should stray (1824)
   Say, sinner, hath a voice within? (1824)

IKELER, Carol Rose (b. 1920). American. Presbyterian

   The churches wherever God's people are praising (1959, 1963)

INGELOW, Jean (1820-1897). British. Church of England

   And didst Thou love the race (1863)

INGLIS, Catherine H. Mahon (1815-1893). British. Church of
   England

   Abide with me. Most loving counsel this (1860)
   Heir of glory, art thou weeping (1864)

IRONS, Genevieve Mary (1855-1928). British. Church of England

   Draw to the Cross which Thou hast blessed (1880)

JANVRIN, Alice Jane (1846-1908). British. Church of England

   Great Jehovah, King of nations (1902)
   He expecteth, He expecteth! (1894)

Lord, I know a work is waiting (1898)
Lord of all the ages of Eternity (1889)

JARVIS, Mary (1853-1929). British. Congregational

O God of ages in whose light (1888)

JEVON, Mary Ann Roscoe (1795-1845). British. Unitarian

O let your mingling voices rise (1845)
Thou must go forth alone, my soul (1845)
When human hopes and joys depart (1820)

JOHNSON, Catherine Hardenbergh (b. 1835). American. Presby-
    terian

An earthly temple here we build (1866)
The whole wide world for Jesus (1872)
We are so happy, God's own little flock (n.d.)

JONES, Edith (1849-1929)

Father, who art alone (1885)

JORDAN, Diane Owen. American. Baptist

O God, our Father, Ruler of the nations (1975)

JOSEPH, Jane M. (1894-1929)

*On this day earth shall ring (n.d.)

JUDSON, Emily Chubbuck ["Fanny Forester"] (1817-1854).
    American. Baptist

(Various hymns in Burmese for the Baptist mission there)

JUDSON, Sarah Hull (1803-1845). American. Baptist

Proclaim the lofty praise (1829)

KENNEY, Alice P. American. Presbyterian

Creator God, whose glory is Creation (1970)

KIDDER, Mary Ann Pepper (1820-1905). American. Methodist
   Episcopal

I care not for riches (1878)
We shall sleep, but not forever (1878)

KIMBALL, Harriet McEwan (1834-1905). American. Roman Catholic

Hymns (1866)

At times on Tabor's height (1866)
Dear Lord, to Thee alone (1866)
It is an easy thing to say (1866)
Jesus, the Ladder of my faith (1866)
Pour Thy blessings, Lord (1866)
We have no tears Thou wilt not dry (1864)

KINNEY, Elizabeth Clementine Dodge (1810-1889). American

Jesus, Saviour, pass not by (1880)

KLINGEMANN, Sophie

*Bells are ringing, birds are singing (1869)
*Can you tell the countless number (1869)
*Every year that endeth (1869)
*From His heaven above (1869)
*The love of Christ makes ever glad (1869)

KNIGHT, Ellis Cornelia

Prayers and Hymns from the German (1812)

*A few short days of trial past (1812)
*Father! from Thee my grateful heart (1812)
*Grant me, O God! a tender heart (1812)

LAMB, Martha (1761-1836). British. Moravian

Glory to our great Creator (1805)

LANCASTER, Mary Ann Elizabeth Shorey (b. 1851). British.
    Church of England

    I have a friend so precious (1890)
    Think of Jesus in the morning (1900)
    Walking with Jesus day by day (1894)

LARCOM, Lucy (1824-1893). American

    At the Beautiful Gate, and Other Songs of Faith (1892)

    Breaks the joyful Easter dawn (1885)
    Draw Thou, my soul, O Christ (1892)
    Hand in hand with angels (1869)
    If the world seems cold to you (1869)
    In Christ I feel the heart of God (1881)
    Heavenly Helper, friend divine (1885)
    O God, Thy world is sweet with prayer (1892)
    O Spirit, whose name is the Saviour (1881)
    Open your hearts as a flower to the light (1892)
    Ring, happy bells of Easter time (1892)

LATHBURY, Mary Artemesia (1841-1918). American. Methodist

    Break thou the bread of life (1880, 1884)
    Day is dying in the west (1880, 1884)
    Lift up, lift up thy voice with singing (1878)

LEE, Dorothy K.

    For this new morning with its light (1959)
    It is Thanksgiving time again (1959)
    Teach me the ways of thankfulness (1959)
    The days and weeks and months pass by (1959)

LEE, Elvira Louisa Ostrehan (1838-1890). British. Church of
    England

    Starry hosts are gleaming (1884)

LEEFE, Isabella (1831-1902). British

    Cantica Sanctorum (1880, 1883)

    Loving Father, throned in glory (1903)
    O Father, ere the night draw near (1903)
    O Jesu, Thou art present (1880)
    The clouds of night have rolled away (1903)

LEESON, Jane Eliza (1807-1882). British. Catholic Apostolic

Hymns and Scenes of Childhood (1842)
Paraphrases and Hymns for Congregational Singing (1853)

A little child may know (1842)
*As rain and snow on earth bestow (1853)
Behold, according to Thy word (1853)
*Christ the Lord is risen today (1853)
Dear Saviour, to Thy little lambs (1842)
Father, I love Thy house of prayer (1842)
Gracious Saviour, gentle Shepherd (1842)
Have ye counted the cost? (1848)
In the dark and silent night (1848)
Jesus Christ, my Lord and King (1842)
King of saints and King of glory (1853)
*Loving Shepherd of Thy sheep (1842)
Now lettest Thou Thy servant, Lord (1853)
Saviour, teach me day by day (1842)
Songs of glory fill the sky (1864)
Stand we prepared to see and hear (1864)
Sweet the lesson Jesus taught (1842)
The days of old were days of might (1848)
Their hearts shall not be moved (1842)
*Wail ye not, but requiems sing (1842)
Wake the song, O Zion's daughter (n.d.)
Wake, ye saints, the song of triumph (1861, 1864)

LESLIE, Mary Eliza (b. 1834). British (b. India). Baptist

They are gathering homeward from every land (1861)

LEYDA, Ida F. American. Presbyterian

In the early morning (n.d.)

LIVERMORE, Sarah White (1789-1874). American. Unitarian

Glory to God and peace on earth (1844)
Our pilgrim brethren, dwelling far (1844)

LIVOCK, Jane Elizabeth (b. 1840). British. Congregational

My soul awake! Thy rest forsake (1880)

LOWE, Helen

    *I know not what I could desire (1841)
    *I say to everyone, He lives (1844)
    *If I have only Him (1841)
    *In many a form I see Thee oft (1841)
    *Of all the golden hours whose light (1841)
    *Tho' all men's faith had banished (1841)
    *What might I not have been without Thee (1841)

LUKE, Jemima Thompson (1813-1906). British. Congregational

    I think when I read that sweet story of old (1841, 1853)

LUNN, Caroline Sophia Grundy (1822-1893). British. Unitarian

    Day and night the blessings fall (1880)

MACALISTER, Edith Florence Boyle (1873-1950). Irish. Pres-
    byterian

    Father, hear us as we pray (1914)
    Lord Jesus, be Thou with us now (1914)

MACDONALD, Mary MacDougall (1789-1872). Scottish. Baptist

    Child in the manger, infant of Mary (n.d.)

MACE, Frances P. Laughton (b. 1836). American

    Only waiting till the shadows (1854)

MACKAY, Margaret (1802-1887). Scottish. Presbyterian

    Asleep in Jesus! blessed steed (1832)

MACRAE, Catherine

    *A Lamb goes forth--for all the dues (1872)

MADAN, Judith Cowper. British. Church of England

    In this world of sin and sorrow (1763)

MANINGTON, Alice.   British

> *Footprints from the Holy Deed: Translations from the German*
>   (1863)
> *A Wreath of Carols from the Fatherland* (1864)

*A stilly angel wanders (1863)
*Adam did, in Paradise (1864)
*Because I see red tints adorning (1863)
*Blessed Jesus, we are here (1863)
*Come, and let us Christ revere now (1864)
*Come God, Creator, Holy Ghost (1863)
*Earth has nothing bright for me (1863)
*From heaven angel hosts did fly (1864)
*From out my woe I cry to Thee (1863)
*Go out my heart, and pleasure seek (1863)
*God cares for me; why need I sorrow (1863)
*Hallelujah! beauteous morning (1863)
*Heaven, earth, land, and sea (1863)
*Help, Jesus, help! in woe, in need (1863)
*Here is Immanuel! (1864)
*I am tired, and so I seek (1863)
*I come, O Lord, and seek for Thee (1863)
*I know that my Redeemer lives (1863)
*I'll sing to Thee with heart and mouth (1863)
*It is evening, and the hour, Lord (1863)
*It is, indeed, a precious thing (1863)
*Jerusalem, thou city rear'd on high (1863)
*Jesus, come Thyself to me (1864)
*Jesus, help conquer, Thou Prince of my being (1863)
*Morning glance of verity (1863)
*My God, again the morning breaketh (1863)
*My God, Thou hast the invite given (1863)
*My heart awakes with holy glee (1863)
*My Saviour lives, and He the might (1863)
*Night from the earth is wending (1863)
*Now every greenwood sleepeth (1863)
*Now heavy heart, away with sorrow (1863)
*Now soon I shall have conquer'd (1863)
*Now that the day from earth hath crept (1863)
*O faithful Saviour, Jesus Christ (1863)
*O Jesus Christ, my sunshine (1864)
*O Jesus Christ, Thy cradle is (1864)
*Oh! love that did the heavens rend asunder (1864)
*Out from the east, the golden morn is rising (1863)
*Praise God, now Christians, all alike (1864)
*Rejoice, that rest is not far distant (1863)
*See! what wondrous love, how matchless (1863)
*Soon night the world in gloom will sleep (1863)
*The autumn is returning (1863)

*The Lord He is my Shepherd kind (1863)
*The week at length is over (1863)
*The woes that weigh my body down (1863)
*The wonderful blessed leadings of God (1863)
*Thou treasure of all treasures (1863)
*Thou Who'rt One, and yet as three (1863)
*Throw, soul, I say, thy fears away (1864)
*Throw the glorious gates wide open (1863)
*Up! Christian man, and join the fight (1863)
*Wake up, my heart, the night has flown (1863)
*When I, Creator, view Thy might (1863)
*Where wilt thou go? (1863)
*Who are those round God's throne standing (1863)
*Who can my soul from Jesus sever (1863)
*Word by God the Father spoken (1863)

MARCY, Elizabeth Eunice (b. 1822). American. Methodist Epis-
    copal

    Out of the depths to Thee I cry (1877)

MARSTON, Annie Wright (b. 1852). British

    I thank Thee, Lord, that Thou hast shown (1890)
    It shall be now (1890)
    Lord, I come at last to Thee (1890)
    Now the Lord our souls has fed (1899)
    O Lord, I come to Thee (1890)
    This day the Lord has spoken (1890)

MARTIN, Civilla D. (1868-1948)

    Be not dismayed whate'er betide (1905)

MARTINEAU, Harriet (1802-1876). British. Unitarian

    All men are equal in their birth (1831)
    Beneath this starry arch (1841)
    Lord Jesus! come; for here (1831)
    The floods of grief have spread around (1831)
    The sun had set, the infant slept (1837)
    What hope was Thine, O Christ! (1831)
    When Samuel heard, in still mid-night (1831)

MASON, Caroline Atherton Briggs (1823-1890).   American.   Unitarian

    I cannot walk in darkness (1875)
    O God, I thank Thee for each night (1875)
    The changing years, eternal God (1884)

MASSEY, Lucy Fletcher (b. 1842).   British.   Church of England

    Hymns on the Imitation of Christ (1871)
    Songs of the Unseen Hope (1900)

    Sweet day of worship, day of rest (1870)

MASTERS, Mary.   British

    Be the living God my friend (1755)
    O my adored Redeemer! deign to be (1755)
    'Tis religion that can give (1755)

MATHESON, Annie (1853-1924).   British.   Congregational

    Dear Master, what can children do? (1882)
    How shall we worship Thee, O Lord? (1882)
    I am weak and weary, Lord (1869)
    Jesus, the children are calling (1866)
    Lord, when we have not any light (1880)
    O little birds, that all day long (1880)
    The little snowdrops rise (1880)
    What is the name of the Lord God Almighty? (1905)
    When there is peace (1905)
    When through life's dewy fields we go (1880)

MAUDE, Mary Fawler Hooper (1819-1913).   British.   Church of England

    Thine for ever, God of love (1847, 1848)

MAURICE, Jane (1812-1892).   Welsh.   Church of England

    Glory to God, for the day-spring is dawning (1861)
    No evil shall befall (1861)
    There is a rest from sin and sorrow (1861)

MAXWELL, Mary Hamlin (1814-1853).   American

    Original Hymns (1849)

God hath said, "For ever blessed" (1849)
Saints of God! the dawn is brightening (1849)

MAY, Catherine Elizabeth Martin (1808-1873).   British.   Church
    of England

O Saviour, where shall guilty man (1858)

McCAW, Mabel Niedermeyer

God is the loving Father (1944)
Our church proclaims God's love and care (1939)
We thank Thee, God, our Father (1943)

McCULLOUGH, Betty

Jesus, our loving friend (1959)
The Bible tells of God's great plan (1959)

McKEEVER, Harriet Burn (1807-1887).   American.   Episcopal

Twilight Musings (1857)

Jesus, high in glory (1847)

MILES, Elizabeth Appleton (1807-1877).   American.   Unitarian

Father, direct my ways (1846)
The earth is all light and loveliness (1828)
Thou who didst stoop below (1827)
When on devotion's seraph wing (1828)

MILLER, Emily Huntington (1833-1913).   American.   Methodist
    Episcopal

Beyond the dark river of death (n.d.)
Blessed are the children (1868)
Enter Thy temple, glorious King (1861)
Father, while the shadows fall (1868)
Hark, the chorus swelling (1868)
I love to hear the story (1867)
Work and never weary (1868)

MILLS, Elizabeth King (1805-1829). British. Church of England
    We speak of the realms of the blest (1829, 1869)

MILNER-BARRY, Alda (1877-1941). British. Church of England
    Good Joseph had a garden (1926)

MITCHELL, Elizabeth Harcourt Rolls (b. 1833). Welsh
    As Abel brought the lamb to Thee (1884)
    As Hebrew children strewed their plains (1881)
    Come to the manger in Bethlehem (1881)
    Good news from the hills of Judea (1881)
    In the desert all alone (1881)
    Jesus, glorious Prince of angels (1884)
    King of glory, Saviour dear (1881)
    Lamb most holy, King most lowly (1884)

MOORE, Jessie Eleanor (1886-1969). American. Methodist
    Our thoughts go round the world (1963)

MORGAN, Mrs. J.P.
    *Forsake me not! O Thou, my Lord, my Light (1883)

MORRIS, Eliza Fanny Goffe (1821-1874). British
    Bible Class Hymn Book (n.d.)

    Come unto me and rest (1858)
    God of pity, God of grace (1858)
    O Thou blest Lamb of God (1858)

MOULE, Harriot Mary Elliott (b. 1844). British. Church of
    England
    Cast thou thy care upon the Lord (1896)

MOULTRIE, Mary Dunlop (d. 1866)
    Agnes fair martyr (1866)
    *Holy night! calmly bright (1867)

MOZLEY, Harriet Newman (d. 1852). British. Church of England
  Hymns for Children on the Lord's Prayer (1835; 6th ed.,
    1856)

  Think upon Eve and Adam's sin (1835)
  When safely on dry land once more (1835)

MUNGER, Harriet Osgood (1857-1925). American. Congregational
  O my Father, I would know Thee (1894)

NICHOLSON, Mary Ann
  Easter flowers are blooming bright (1875)

NOEL, Caroline Maria (1817-1877). British. Church of England
  At the name of Jesus (1870)
  Draw nigh unto my soul (1834)

NUNN, Marianne (1778-1847). British. Church of England
  One there is above all others (1817)

OAKEY, Emily Sullivan (1829-1883)
  I am so glad that our Father in heaven (n.d.)

OGDON, Ina Duley (1872-1964). American. Christian Church
  Brighten the corner where you are (1912)
  Carry your cross with a smile (n.d.)

OGLEVEE, Louise M. McAvoy (1872-1953). American. Presbyterian
  This is God's holy house (1950)

OPIE, Amelia Alderson (1769-1853). British. Quaker
  There seems a voice in every gale (1802)
  When the disciples saw their Lord (1838)

OSSOLI, Sarah Margaret Fuller (1810-1850). American. Unitarian

    Jesus, a child His course began (1859)

OWENS, Priscilla Jane (1829-1907). American. Methodist Episcopal

    We have heard a joyful sound (1898)
    Will your anchor hold in the storms of life? (n.d.)

PAGE, Kate Stearns (1873-1963)

    We, Thy people, praise Thee, praise Thee (n.d.)

PALMER, Alice Freeman (1855-1902). American. Congregational

    How sweet and silent is the place (1901)

PALMER, Phoebe (1807-1874). American. Methodist

    Blessed Bible! how I love thee (n.d.)
    O! when shall I sweep through the gates (1878)

PARR, Harriet (1828-1900). British

    Hear my prayer, O heavenly Father (1856)

PARSON, Elizabeth Rooker (1812-1873). British. Congregational

    Angels round the throne are praising (1840)
    Far above the lofty sky (1858)
    Father of spirits, we entreat (1858)
    Hark! 'tis the Saviour calls (1858)
    Is there one heart, dear Saviour, here (1858)
    Jesus, we love to meet (1858)
    Lord, we bend before Thee now (1858)
    O happy land, O happy land (1840)
    Our Saviour's voice is soft and sweet (1858)
    Saviour, round Thy footstool bending (1840)
    This is God's most holy day (n.d.)
    Youthful, weak, and unprotected (1858)

PEARCE, Lydia Freeman Moser (b. 1841). British. Church of England

    In the hollow of His hand (n.d.)
    O Son of Man! Great Sower (1893)

PEARCE, Selina P. (b. 1845). American. Baptist

  Be our joyful song today (n.d.)
  Hark, 'tis the voice of gladness (n.d.)

PENNEFATHER, Catherine King (d. 1893). British. Church of
    England

  I'm journeying through a desert world (1873)
  Not now, my child; a little more rough tossing (1873)

PERKINS, Emily S. American

  Stonehurst Hymn Tunes (1921)

  Thou art, O God, the God of might (1921)

PETERS, Mary Bowly (1813-1856). British. Church of England

  Hymns Intended To Help the Communion of Saints (1847)

  Around Thy table, Holy Lord (1842)
  Blessed Lord, our hearts are parting (1842)
  Earth's firmest ties will perish (1847)
  Enquire, my soul, enquire (1847)
  Hallelujah, we are hastening (1847)
  Holy Father, we address Thee (1847)
  How can there be one holy thought! (1842)
  Jesus! how much Thy name unfolds (1842)
  Jesus, of Thee we ne'er would tire (1847)
  Lord Jesus, in Thy name alone (1847)
  Lord, through the desert drear and wide (1847)
  Lord, we see the day approaching (1842)
  Many sons to glory bring (1847)
  O Lord, we know it matters not (1842)
  O Lord, whilst we confess the worth (1847)
  Our God is light, we do not go (1847)
  Praise ye the Lord, again, again (1847)
  Salvation to our God (1847)
  The holiest we enter (1847)
  The murmurs of the wilderness (1842)
  The saints while dispersed abroad (1842)
  Through the love of God our Saviour (1847)
  Thy grace, O Lord, to us hath shown (1847)
  Unworthy is thanksgiving (1842)
  We're pilgrims in the wilderness (1847)

Whom have we, Lord, but Thee (1842)
With thankful hearts, we meet, O Lord (1842)

PETRE, Lady Katherine Howard (1831-1882). British. Roman
Catholic

Behold the handmaid of the Lord (1864)
Bow down, my soul, for He hath bowed (1864)
Dry your tears, ye silent mourners (1864)
Love, thou dost all excel (1864)
Steep is the hill, and weary is the road (1864)

PHILLIPS, Edna Martha (b. 1904). Scottish. Presbyterian

Teach me to serve Thee, Lord (1964)

PHILLIPS, Harriet Cecilia (1806-1884). American. Methodist
Episcopal

We bring no glittering treasures (1848, 1849)

PIGOTT, Jean Sophia (1845-1882). Irish. Evangelical Christian
(Keswick Movement)

Jesus, I am resting, resting (1875)

POLLARD, Adelaide A. (1862-1934)

Have Thine own way, Lord! (1902)

POLLARD, Josephine (b. 1840). American

I stood outside the gate (1878)
Joy-bells ringing, children singing (1878)

POPPLE, Maria (1796-1847). British. Unitarian

Restore, O Father, to our times restore (1837)

PRENTISS, Elizabeth Payson (1818-1878). American. Presbyterian

As on a vast eternal shore (1869)
More love to Thee, O Christ (1869, 1872)

PRESTON, Mrs. M.J.   American

   *O that day, that day of ire (1851)

PRICE, Marion James.   American.   Episcopal

   O Jesus, who once heard the plea (1961)
   The church of Christ has work to do (1970)

PROCTER, Adelaide Anne (1825-1864).   British.   Roman Catholic

   I do not ask, O Lord, that life may be (1862)
   I thank Thee, O my God, Who made (1858)
   One by one the sands are going (1858)
   Rise, for the day is passing (1858)
   Strive, yet I do not promise (1858)
   The shadows of the evening hours (1862)
   We ask for peace, O Lord (1858)

PYPER, Mary (1795-1870).   British

   We shall see Him, in our nature (1847)

REED, Edith Margaret Gellibrand (1885-1935).   British

   *Infant holy, infant lowly (1926)

REED, Eliza Holmes (1794-1867).   British.   Congregational

   Gracious Lord, as Thou hast bidden (1842)
   I would be Thine, O take my heart (1842)
   O do not let the word depart (1842)
   O that I could for ever dwell (1842)

RHODES, Sarah Betts (1829-1904).   British.   Congregational

   God, who made the earth (1870, 1879)

RICE, Caroline Laura (b. 1819)

   Wilt thou hear the voice of praise (n.d.)

RICHARDSON, Charlotte (1775-1825).   British

   O God, to Thee we raise our eyes (1804)

RICHTER, Anne Rigby (d. 1857). British. Church of England

    We have not seen Thy footsteps tread (1841)

ROBERTS, Katharine Emily (1877-1962). British. Church of England

    *All poor men and humble (1928)

ROBERTS, Martha Susan Blakeney (b. 1862). British. Church of England

    Be present, Holy Father, to bless our work today (1880, 1881)
    O Saviour Christ, Who art Thyself (1882)
    Rise, O British nation, hasten now to pay (1886)

ROSSETTI, Christina Georgiana (1830-1894). British. Church of England

    A burdened heart that bleeds and bears (1885)
    Give me the lowest place (1866)
    God the Father, give us grace (1865)
    I bore with thee long weary days and nights (1862)
    I would have gone, God bade me stay (1866)
    In the bleak midwinter (1872)
    None other Lamb, none other Name (1892)
    Once I thought to sit so high (1863)
    The Advent moon shines cold and clear (1862)
    The flowers that bloom in sun and shade (1881)
    The shepherds had an angel (1856)
    We know not a voice of that river (1892)
    What are these that glow from afar? (1865)

ROWAN, Frederica M.

    *If I trust in God alone (1862)

ROWE, Elizabeth Singer (1674-1737). British. Independent

    Hymns and Versions of the Psalms (1739)

ROWLAND, May (1870-1959)

    The day is slowly wending (n.d.)

SAFFERY, Maria Grace Horsey (1773-1858). British. Baptist

Poems on Sacred Subjects (1834)

Fain, O my babe, I'd have Thee know (1844)
God of the sunlight hours, how sad (1834)
There is a little lonely fold (1834)
'Tis the great Father we adore (1817, 1828)

SANGSTER, Margaret E. (1838-1912). American. Congregational-
    Dutch Reformed

O Christ, forget not them who stand (n.d.)

SAXBY, Jane Euphemia Browne (1811-1898). British. Church of
    England

Father, into Thy loving hands (1849)
O Jesus Christ, the holy One (1867)
O Holy Ghost, the comforter (1849)
Shew me the way, O Lord (1849)
Thou art with me, O my Father (n.d.)
Thou God of love, beneath Thy sheltering wings (1849)

SCOTT, Clara H. (1841-1897)

Open my eyes, that I may see (1895)

SCOTT, Elizabeth (1708-1776). British-American. Congregational

All hail, Incarnate God (1769)
Awake, our drowsy souls (1769)
Dare we indulge to wrath and strife (1740)
Eternal Spirit, 'twas Thy breath (1740)
For ever shall my fainting soul (1740)
God of my life, to Thee belongs (1769)
Great God, Thy penetrating eye (1740)
My God, shall I for ever mourn? (1769)
See how the rising sun (1806)
The glittering spangles of the sky (1740)
The Lord of love will sure indulge (1769)
Thy bounties, gracious Lord (1740)
When Abram full of sacred awe (1769)
Where'er the Lord shall build my house (1740)
Why, O my heart, those anxious cares? (1769)

SCUDDER, Eliza (1821-1896). American. Unitarian-Protestant
    Episcopal

   Hymns and Sonnets (1897)

   From past regret and present feebleness (1871)
   I cannot find Thee! still on restless pinion (1864)
   In Thee my powers and treasures live (1855, 1864)
   Let whoever will enquire (1855)
   Life of our life, and light of all our seeing! (1875)
   The day is done! the weary day of thought and toil is past
     (1874, 1878)
   Thou grace divine, encircling all (1852, 1857)
   Thou hast gone up again (1880)
   Thou long disowned, reviled, opprest (1864)

SHAPCOTE, Emily Mary Steward (1829-1909). British. Roman
    Catholic

   Hymns for Infant Children (1852)

   Heavenly Father, from Thy throne (1852)
   Jesus, holy, undefiled (1852)
   O Jesus, dearest Lord, I cry to Thee (1876)
   Queen of the Holy Rosary (1882)

SHEKLETON, Mary (1827-1883). Irish

   It passeth knowledge (1863)
   One fervent wish, my God (1867)

SHELLY, Martha Evans Jackson (1812-1901). British

   Father, let Thy benediction (1844)
   Lord, a little band and lowly (1844)
   Lord, help us as we sing (1886)

SHEPHERD, Anne Houlditch (1809-1857). British. Church of
    England

   Hymns adapted to the Comprehension of Young Minds (1847,
    1855)

   Around the throne of God in heaven thousands of children
     (c. 1838)
   Glory to Jesus, glory (1847)
   Here's a message of love (1847)
   I have read of the Saviour's love (1847)
   See where the gentle Jesus reigns (1847)

SHIELDS, Elizabeth McEwan (1879-1962). American. Presbyterian

    I like to think of Jesus (1958)

SHIPTON, Anna (1815-1901). British

    The Brook in the Way. Original Hymns (1864)
    Whispers in the Palms. Hymns and Meditations (1855, 1857)

    Call them in, the poor, the wretched (1862)
    Down in the pleasant pastures (1855)
    Father, my cup is full (1855)
    How shall I praise Thee, O my God? (1855)
    Jesus, Master, hear my cry (1855)
    Praise God, ye gladdening smiles of morn (n.d.)

SIDNEY, Mary, Countess of Pembroke (1550-1621). British.
    Church of England

    The Psalmes of David, Translated into Divers and Sundry
    Kinds of Verse. . . . Begun by the Noble and Learned
    Gent., Sir Philip Sidney, Knt., and Finished by the
    Right Honourable the Countess of Pembroke, His Sister
    (pub. 1823)

SIGOURNEY, Lydia Huntley (1791-1865). American. Baptist

    Blest Comforter divine (1824)
    Choose ye His Cross to bear (1829)
    Go to thy rest, my child (1841)
    Labourers of Christ, arise (1836)
    Little raindrops feed the rill (1841)
    Lord, may the spirit of this feast (1845)
    Not for the summer hour alone (1841)
    Onward, onward, men of heaven (1833)
    Pastor, thou art from us taken (1836)
    Prayer is the dew of faith (n.d.)
    Saviour, Thy law we love (1832)
    There was a noble ark (1841)
    We mourn for those who toil (1831)
    We praise Thee if one rescued soul (1846)
    We thank Thee, Father, for the day (1850)
    When adverse winds and waves arise (1823)
    When the parting bosom bleeds (1846)
    Where wilt thou put thy trust? (1845)

SIMPSON, Jane Cross Bell (1811-1886). Scottish. Presbyterian

>   Go when the morning shineth (1831)
>   I had a lesson to teach them (1867)
>   Star of morning, brightly shining (1878)
>   Star of peace to wanderers weary (1830, 1878)

SKEMP, Ada (1857-1927). British. Baptist

>   I love to think that Jesus saw (1908)

SLADE, Mary B.C. (1826-1882)

>   From all the dark places of earth's needy races (n.d.)

SMITH, Caroline Louisa Sprague (1827-1886). American. Con-
    gregational

>   Tarry with me, O my Saviour (1852, 1855)

SMITH, Elizabeth Lee Allen (1817-1898). American

>   *I greet Thee, who my sure Redeemer art (1869)
>   *O Jesus Christ, grow Thou in me (1860)

SMITH, Florence Margaret (1886-1958). British. Church of
    England

>   Lord and Master, who hast called us (1913)

SMITH, Mrs. L.C.

>   *Dear Lord, to hear Thee and Thy word (1873)
>   *O how blest who, all resigning (1865)

SOUTHEY, Caroline Ann Bowles (1786-1854). British. Church
    of England

>   I weep, but not rebellious tears (1826)
>   Launch thy bark, mariner (1826)

SPAETH, Mrs. H.R. American. Lutheran

>   *As each happy Christmas (1885)
>   *Church bells ring (1885)

*Glory to God upon His throne (1883)
*Lo, on a mount a tree doth stand (1885)
*Whom Jesus loves (1883)

STEAD, Louisa M.R. (1850-1917)

'Tis so sweet to trust in Jesus (n.d.)

STEELE, Anne (1716-1778). British. Baptist

Ah, wretched souls who strive in vain (1760)
Ah, wretched, vile, ungrateful heart (1760)
Alas! what hourly dangers rise (1760)
Almighty Author of my frame (1760)
Almighty Father, gracious Lord (1760)
Amazing love that stoop'd so low (1760)
And can my heart aspire so high (1780)
And did the Holy and the Just (1760)
And is the gospel peace and love? (1760)
And will the Lord thus condescend (1760)
Awake, awake, the sacred song (1760)
Awake, my soul, awake my tongue (1760)
Blest be the Lord, our strength and shield (1760)
Bright scenes of bliss, unclouded skies (1760)
Come, heavenly love, inspire my song (1760)
Come, Lord, and warm each languid heart (1760)
Come, Thou desire of all Thy saints (1760)
Come weary souls, with sin distressed (1760)
Dear refuge of my weary soul (1760)
Dear Saviour, when my thoughts recall (1780)
Far from these narrow scenes of night (1760)
Father of mercies, in Thy word (1760)
Forgive, blest shade, the tributary tear (1760)
Great God, this sacred day of Thine (1760)
Great Ruler of the earth and skies (1760)
He lives! the great Redeemer lives (1760)
Hence, vain intruding world, depart (1760)
Jesus demands this heart of mine (1760)
Jesus, Thou source divine (1760)
Lord, how mysterious are Thy ways (1760)
Lord, how shall wretched sinners dare (1780)
Lord, in Thy great, Thy glorious Name (1760)
Lord of my life, O may Thy praise (1760)
My God, my Father, blissful name (1760)
My God, 'tis to Thy mercy-seat (1760)
My Maker and my King; to Thee my whole I owe (1760)
See, gracious God, before Thy throne (1756, 1760)

The Lord forgets His wonted grace (1760)
The Lord, my Saviour, is my Light (1760)
When blooming youth is snatched away (1760)
When I resolved to watch my thoughts (1760)
When I survey life's varied scene (1760)
While justice waves her vengeful hand (1757, 1760)
Ye wretched, hungry, starving poor (1760)

STEVENSON, Isabel Stephana (1843-1890). British. Church of
    England

    Holy Father! in Thy mercy (1889)

STEVENSON, Lilian (1870-1960). Irish. Presbyterian

    *Fairest Lord Jesus (1924)

STEVENSON, Matilda Boyle Davis (b. 1838). British. Congrega-
    tional

    Sweet flowers are blooming in God's sight (1880)

STOCK, Sarah Geraldine (1838-1898). British. Church of England

    A cry as of pain (1890, 1891)
    A debtor! for the love of God unbounded (1878)
    Called to Thy service, Lord (1889)
    He shall reign o'er all the earth (n.d.)
    Hear ye not the tramp of reapers? (1889)
    Jesus! all-sufficiency (1882)
    Jesus calls, He it is (1892)
    Let the song go round the earth (1898, 1899)
    Lord of light, and Fount of love (1875)
    Lord of love, and truth, and grace (n.d.)
    Lord, Thy ransomed Church is waking (1874)
    O Master! when Thou callest (1888)
    O when shall their souls find a rest? (1893)
    Once Thy servants toiled in rowing (1892)
    Open stood the gates of heaven (n.d.)
    Round Thy footstool, Saviour, see (1896)
    Shut out from heaven's glory (n.d.)
    Someone shall go at the Master's word (1893)
    The love of Christ constraining (1891)
    The tender light of home behind (1887)
    There's a fight to be fought, there's a work to be done
        (1888)
    They are waiting everywhere (1893)

Thy servants, Lord, are dear to Thee (n.d.)
Treasures we have gathered here (1896)
We are children of the King (1891)
We know not how the rays that stream (1868)
With voice of joy and singing (1887)

STOCKTON, Martha Matilda Brustar (1821-1885). American

God loved the world of sinners lost (1871)

STONE, Mary Kent Adams (b. 1835). American. Protestant Episcopal

Lord, with a very tired mind (1879)

STOWE, Harriet Beecher (1811-1896). American. Congregational

Knocking, knocking, who is there? (1867)
How beautiful, said he of old (1864)
Still, still with Thee, when purple morning breaketh (1855)
That mystic word of Thine, O sovereign Lord (1855)
When winds are raging o'er the upper ocean (1855)

STRAFFORD, Elizabeth (1828-1868). British

God Almighty, heareth ever (1857)
Once to our world there came (1857)
We praise Thee, we bless Thee (1857)

STREATFEILD, Charlotte Saint (b. 1829). British. Church of England

Hymns and Verses on the Collects (1865)
Hymns on the Love of Jesus, and the Home Above (1877)

And didst Thou hunger then, O Lord (1865)
Brothers, tread the holy portals (n.d.)
He scarcely felt the cruel stones (1865)
High o'er the glittering temple (1881)
How beautiful the hills of God (1881)
I linger round the fold of God (1885)
In the Paradise of Jesus (1877)
Jesus, tender Shepherd, seeking for Thine own (1885)
Sweet Shepherd, Thou hast sought me (1877)
There is joy amongst the angels (1877)

Harriet Beecher Stowe. From Albert Edward Bailey. *The Gospel in Hymns. Backgrounds and Interpretations.* New York: Charles Scribner's Sons, 1950, p. 497. ". . . portrait made in England"

STUTSMAN, Grace M. (b. 1886)

In Bethlehem near starlit skies (1963)

TAYLOR, Clare. British. Church of England-Moravian

All glory be to God on high (1742)
Behold the loving Son of God (1742)
Lord, my times are in Thy hand (1789)
Lord, to Thy people and dispense (1789)
O Jesus, Jesus, my good Lord (1742)
O Lord, the contrite sinner's Friend (1742)
Our heavenly Father is not known (1742)
The Cross, the Cross, Oh that's my gain (1742)
What praise unto the Lamb is due (n.d.)
Who can condemn, since Christ hath died? (1742)

TAYLOR, Emily (1795-1872). British. Unitarian-Church of
    England

Come to the house of prayer (1818)
God of the changing year (1818)
Here, Lord, when at Thy table met (1826)
If love, the noblest, purest, blest (1837)
O Father, though the anxious fear (1818)
O here, if ever, God of love (1818)
O not for these alone I pray (1826)
O source of good! around me spread (1826)
The Gospel is the light (1826)
Thus shalt thou love the Almighty God (1826)
Truly the light of morn is sweet (1826)
When summer suns their radiance fling (1826)
Who shall behold the King of Kings? (1826)
Who that o'er many a barren part (1826)

TAYLOR, Helen (1818-1885). British

Missionary Hymns for the Use of Children (1846)

A feather'd seed that lifted is (1846)
And shall we dwell together (1846)
Father, the little offering take (1846)
I love that Holy Scripture (n.d.)
There is a happy land on high (1846)

TAYLOR, Jane (1783-1824). British. Congregational

A sinner, Lord, behold I stand (1809)
Almighty God, Who dwellest high (1809)
Come, my fond, fluttering heart (1812)
Death has been here, and borne away (1816)
God is so good that He will hear (1809)
God!--What a great and awful name (1809)
How dreadful to be turned away (1812)
Jesus Christ, my Lord and Saviour (1810)
Lord, I would own Thy tender care (1809)
Love and kindness we may measure (1809)
Now condescend, Almighty King (1809)
Now that my journey's just begun (1810)
O Lord, wilt Thou teach me to pray? (1813)
There is a path that leads to God (1810)
This is a precious book indeed (1809)
What is there, Lord, a child can do? (n.d.)
When daily I kneel down to pray (1809)
When for some little insult given (1809)
When to the house of God we go (1809)
Young children once to Jesus came (1810)

TAYLOR, Rebekah Hope Morley (d. 1877). British. Plymouth
        Brethren

Blessed Saviour, I would praise Thee (1873)
My Saviour, I would own Thee (1873)
One more boundary passed o'er (1873)
Thou art the way, O Lord (1873)

TAYLOR, Sarah Ellen (1883-1954)

O God of light, Thy Word (1952)

THOBURN, Helen (1885-1932)

Father of lights, in whom there is no shadow (n.d.)

THOMSON, Mary Ann Faulkner (1834-1923). American (b. England).
        Episcopalian

Lo! amid the shades of night (1891)
Now the blessed dayspring (1890)
O King of saints, we give (1890)
O Sion, haste, Thy mission high fulfilling (1892)
Saviour, for the little one (1892)

THRELFALL, Jeannette (1821–1880). British.   Church of England

> Hosannah! loud hosannah, the little children sing (1873)
> I think of Thee, O Saviour (1857)
> Lo, to us a child is born (1873)
> Thou bidd'st us to seek Thee early (1873)
> We praise Thee in the morning (1873)
> When from Egypt's house of bondage (1873)

THRUPP, Dorothy Ann (1779–1847). British

> *Hymns for the Young* (1830; 4th ed., 1836)

> A little ship was on the sea (1840)
> A widowed mother lost her son (1840)
> Almighty God, Thy name I praise (1830)
> Come, happy children, come and raise (1830)
> Come, Holy Spirit, come, O hear an infant's prayer (1838)
> God loves the little child that prays (1836)
> Have you read the wondrous story? (1830)
> Let us sing with one accord (1836)
> Poor and needy though I be (1836)
> See, my child, the mighty ocean (1836)
> Thou Guardian of my earliest days (1836)
> What a strange and wondrous story (1836)
> What led the Son of God? (1830)
> Who are they in heaven who stand? (1846)

THWAITES, Clara Hepworth (b. 1839). British.   Church of England

> O world of pride, throw open wide (1887)
> The red cross of our banner (1899)
> The sunset burns across the sky (1890)

TOKE, Emma Leslie (1812–1878).   Irish.   United Church of
    England and Ireland

> Glory to Thee! O Lord, Who from this world of sin (1851,
>   1852)
> Jesu! by whose Almighty grace (1870)
> Lord God, the strength and stay of all (1870)
> Lord, in all our trials here (1852)
> Lord of all power and might (1870)
> Lord of light and life (1870)
> Lord of Thy mercy, hear our cry (1852)
> O Father, whom in truth to know (1870)
> O God of comfort, Thou alone (1870)

O God of mercy, chill and dark (1870)
O God, the strength and stay of all (1870)
O God, upon this solemn day (1870)
O Lord, in all our travels here (1851, 1852)
O Lord, Thou knowest all the snares (1851, 1852)
O Thou, to whose all seeing eye (1852)
O Thou, Who didst through heavens (1870)
O Thou, Who didst with love untold (1851, 1852)
The joyful day at last is come (1870)
This is the day when Jesus Christ (1870)
Thou art gone up on high (1851, 1852)
Upon this sad and solemn day (1870)
We bless Thee, Lord, for that clear light (1870)

TONNA, Charlotte Elizabeth Browne (1790-1846). British.
    Church of England

Holy Father, heavenly King (1832)
O God of Israel, deign to smile (n.d.)
O Thou who didst prepare (1829)
Sinner, what hast thou to show? (1829)
Soldier, go, but not to claim (n.d.)

TORREY, Mary Ide (1817-1869). American

When silent steal across my soul (1857)

TRESTRAIL, Elizabeth Ryland Dent (b. 1813). British. Baptist

Hallelujah! Praise the Lord (1864)

TURNER, Nancy Byrd (b. 1880). American. Episcopal

O Son of man, who walked each day (1928)

TYNAN-HINKSON, Katharine (1861-1931). Irish. Roman Catholic

Thy kingdom come; yea, bid it come (1885)

VAN ALSTYNE, Frances Jane Crosby ["Fanny Crosby"] (1823-1915).
    American. Methodist Episcopal

All the way my Saviour leads me (1875)
Beautiful mansions, home of the blest (1867)
Christ the Lord is risen today (1869)

Come, O come with thy broken heart (1875)
Dark is the night, and cold the wind is blowing (1868)
From my everlasting portion (1874)
Great is Jehovah, King of kings (1871)
Here from the world we turn (1876)
Holy, holy, holy is the Lord! sing O ye people (1869)
How sweet when we mingle (1866, 1875)
I am Jesus' little friend (1873)
I am Thine, O Lord (1875)
I would be Thy little lamb (1871)
If I come to Jesus, He will make me glad (1868)
In Thy cleft, O Rock of Ages (1880)
Jesus I love Thee (1873)
Jesus, keep me near the Cross (1869)
Jesus the water of life has given (1867)
Lead me to Jesus (1871)
Light and comfort of my soul (1867)
Little beams of rosy light (1869)
Lord, at Thy mercy seat (1868)
Lord, my trust I repose on Thee (1877)
Loving Saviour, hear my cry (1873)
Mourner, whereso'er thou art (1871, 1873)
Never be faint or weary (1873)
O come to the Saviour, believe in His name (1874, 1875)
O hear my cry, be gracious now to me (1877)
O my Saviour, hear me (1875)
O what are you going to do, brother? (1868)
Only a step to Jesus (1873)
Only Jesus feels and knows (1875)
Pass me not, O gentle Saviour (1870)
Praise Him, praise Him (1869)
Press on! press on! a glorious throng (1869)
Rescue the perishing, care for the dying (1870)
Revive Thy work, O Lord (1875)
Safe in the arms of Jesus (1868, 1869)
Saviour, bless a little child (1869)
Saviour, more than life for me (1875)
Say, where is thy refuge, my brother? (1874)
Softly on the breath of evening (1864)
Sound the alarm! let the watchman cry (1880)
Sweet hour of prayer (1861)
Tenderly He leads us (1880)
There's a cry from Macedonia (1867)
'Tis the blessed hour of prayer (1880)
To God be the glory, great things He hath done (1875)
To the work, to the work (1871)
'Twill not be long--our journey here (1868)
We are going, we are going (1864)

Frances Jane Crosby Van Alstyne. From Tharon Brown and Hezekiah Butterworth. *The Story of the Hymns and Tunes*. New York: American Tract Society, 1906, p. 302.

We are marching on with shield and banner bright (1867)
When Jesus comes to reward His servants (1876)
Why labour for treasures that rust and decay? (1871)

VILLIERS, Margaret Elizabeth Leigh, Countess of Jersey (b. 1849)
    British. Church of England

Hymns and Poems for Very Little Children (1871, 1875)

Here am I, for Thou didst call me (1871)
Holy Jesus, Who didst die (1871)
I am a little soldier (1871)
O let me praise my God and King (1871)
Speak the truth, for that is right (1871)
There are many lovely things below (1871)

WADDELL, Helen (1889-1965). Irish. Presbyterian

Lover of souls and Lord of all the living (n.d.)

WALKER, Mary Jane Deck (1816-1878). British. Church of
    England-Plymouth Brethren

He came, Whose embassy was peace (1855)
I journey through a desert near and wild (1855)
Jesus, I will trust Thee (1855)
Lord, Thou didst love Jerusalem (1855)
O God, our Saviour, from Thy birth (1855)
O joyful tidings let us sing (1855)
O spotless Lamb of God, in Thee (1855)
The wanderer no more will roam (1855)
We are not left to walk alone (1855)

WARING, Anna Laetitia (1820-1910). Welsh. Church of England

Additional Hymns (1858)
Hymns and Meditations by A.L.W. (1850; 4th ed., 1854; 10th
    ed., 1863)

Dear Saviour of a dying world (1854)
Father, I know that all my life (1850)
Go not far from me, O my strength (1854)
In heavenly love abiding (1850)
Jesus, Lord of Heaven above (1854)
Lord, a happy child of Thine (1850)
My Saviour, on the words of truth (1850)
O this is blessing, this is rest (1854)

O Thou Lord of heaven above (n.d.)
Source of my life's refreshing springs (1850)
Sunlight of the heavenly day (1854)
Sweet is the solace of Thy love (1850)
Tender mercies on my way (1850)
Thanksgiving and the voice of melody (1854)
Though some good things of lower worth (1850)
Under Thy wings, my God, I rest (1850)

WARNER, Anna Bartlett (1820-1915). American. Episcopalian

Hymns for the Church Militant (1858)
Wayfaring Hymns, Original and Translated (1869)

*Another day is ended (1869)
*As God leads me, I will go (1858)
*Be Thou faithful to the end (1858)
*Christ the Lord, in death-bonds lay (1858)
*Come, children! on; this way (1858)
*God doth not leave His own (1858)
*God lives! can I despair (1869)
*Hallelujah! Jesus lives! (1858)
*Heavenward our road doth lie (1858)
*Here am I Lord, Thou callest me (1858)
*How shall I get there? who will aid? (1858)
*I'll not leave Jesus, never, never (1858)
*Jesus, help conquer! my spirit is sinking (1858)
*Jesus is come, O joy heaven-lighted (1858)
*Jesus lives! with Him shall I (1869)
 Jesus loves me, this I know (1859)
*Let love weep--it cometh (1858)
*Lord, make my spirit still (1869)
*Lord, my house of clay (1858)
*Lord, Thou hast bid us labour, bid us toil (1858)
*Love doth the whole--not part--desire (1869)
*My God! I know full well that I must die (1858)
*My God, within Thy hand (1858)
*My Jesus the sinner receives (1869)
*My whole desire doth briefly turn away (1869)
*Not more than I have strength to bear (1858)
*Not so darkly, not so deep (1858)
*Now I live; but if to night (1858)
*O beautiful abode of earth (1858)
*O foolish heart, be still (1858)
 O little child, lie still and sleep (1867)
*O soul, why dost thou weary (1869)
 One more day's work for Jesus (1869)
*See what a man is this, O glances (1869)

*Shall I not trust my God (1858)
*Since I one day from yonder sleeping (1869)
*Thanks, thanks to Thee for Thy pity (1869)
 The world looks very beautiful (1860)
*Thou All-sufficient One! Who art (1858)
*To-day mine, to-morrow Thine (1858)
*What is this that round the throne (1869)
*Whatever God does is well (1858)

WARNER, Susan (1819–1895). American. Episcopalian

Jesus bids us shine with a pure, clear light (1868)

WESTON, Rebecca J.

Father, we thank Thee for the night (1885)

WHITING, Mary Bradford. British. Church of England

Come ye yourselves apart and rest awhile (1882)
Lord of might, our land's defender (1903)
O sun of truth and glory (1882)
O word of love! O word of life (1882)
There was a beauty on the sea (1882)
Time is swiftly passing o'er us (1882)
To mourn our dead we gather here (1903)
To Thee, Creator, in whose love (1882)
What was the holy joy, O Lord (1882)

WHITMORE, Lady Lucy Elizabeth Georgiana (1792–1840). British.
     Church of England

Father, again in Jesus' name we meet (1824)

WHITTEMORE, Hannah M. (1822–1881). British

How sweet to think that all who love (1845)

WIGLESWORTH, Esther (1827–1904). British. Church of England

Almighty Father, God of love (1878)
Father, look upon Thy children (1878)
God chooseth out the place (1878)
God sets a still small voice (1878)
How beautiful is earth (1878)

Little children, Advent bids you (1878)
O Fount of life and beauty (1878)
Thou who with dying lips (1878)
When we in holy worship (1878)

WILE, Frances **Whitmarsh** (1875-1939). American

All beautiful the march of days (1912)

WILKINSON, Kate Barclay (1859-1928). British. Church of
England

May the mind of Christ my Saviour (1912)

WILKINSON, Rebecca

See in the vineyard of the Lord (1795)
See the kind Shepherd, Jesus, stands (1795)

WILLARD, Emma C. Hart (1787-1870). American

Rocked in the cradle of the deep (1830)

WILLIAMS, Helen Maria (1762-1827). British. Presbyterian

My God, all nature owns Thy sway (1786)
While Thee I seek, protecting power (1786)

WILLIAMS, Sarah (1838-1868). British

Because I know not when my life was good (1868)

WILLIAMS, Sarah Johanna (1805-1841). British. Unitarian

Quiet from God! it cometh not to still (1834)

WILLIS, Love Maria Whitcomb (1824-1908). American

Father, hear the prayer I offer (1859)

WILLS, Ruth (b. 1826). British. Congregational

Lays of Lowly Life (1861, 1868)
We meet, we part, how few the hours! (1880)

WILSON, Caroline Fry (1787-1846). British

> For what shall I praise Thee (n.d.)
> Often the clouds of deepest woe (1821)

WILSON, Jane (1836-1872). British. Roman Catholic

> A fast before a feast (1861)
> A virgin heart she brought to Christ (1861)
> Again our Lent has come to us (1861)
> At eventide was light (1861)
> Behold she comes, in silence (n.d.)
> Calms the saint's slumber (n.d.)
> Deep thoughts were in her breast (1861)
> I love the courts of Jesus (1861)
> Jesu, ever present with Thy church below (1861)
> Loud in exultation (1861)
> Love and death have wrestled fiercely (1861)
> 'Midst the bitter waters Moses (1861)
> The Church and world for once (1861)
> 'Tis good, O Jesu, that alone with Thee (n.d.)
> We cry to Thee, O Jesu (1861)
> We hail renouned Alban (1861)

WILSON, Margaret Chalmers Hood (1825-1902). Scottish. Pres-
    byterian (Free Church of Scotland)

> If washed in Jesus' blood (1870)
> We know there's a bright and glorious home (1865)

WINKWORTH, Catherine (1829-1878). British. Church of England

> *Choral Book for England* (1863)
> *Christian Singers of Germany* (1869)
> *Lyra Germanica* (1855, 1858)

> *A dread hath come on me (1863)
> *A pilgrim here I wander (1858)
> *A Ship comes sailing onwards (1869)
> *A spotless rose is blowing (1858)
> *Abide among us with Thy grace (1858)
> *Against Thee only have I sinned (1863)
> *Ah dearest Lord! to feel that Thou art near (1858)
> *Ah God, from heav'n look down (1863)
> *Ah God! the world has nought to please (1869)
> *Ah! Jesu Christ, my Lord most dear (1869)
> *Ah Jesus, the merit (1858)

Catherine Winkworth. From *Hymns Ancient and Modern. Historical Edition*. London: William Clowes and Sons, Ltd., 1909, p. cvii. "From a photograph by J. Fisher, Clifton"

*Ah! Lord, how shall I meet Thee (1863)
*Ah! Lord one God, let them not be confounded (1869)
 Ah, whither flee, or where abide (1865)
*Ah wounded Head! must Thou (1855)
*Ah wounded Head, that bearest (1863)
*Alas, dear Lord, what evil hast Thou done (1855)
*Alas, dear Lord, what law then hast Thou broken (1863)
*Alas for my sorrow (1869)
*Alas! my God! my sins are great (1863)
*All glories of this earth decay (1869)
*All glory be to God on high (1863)
*All my heart this night rejoices (1858)
*All my hope is grounded surely (1863)
*All praise and thanks to God most high (1858)
*All things hang on our possessing (1858)
*All ye Gentile lands awake (1855)
*Am I a stranger here on earth alone (1855)
*Anoint us with Thy blessed love (1869)
*Arise, the Kingdom is at hand (n.d.)
*As a bird on meadows fair (1858)
*At dead of night sleep took her flight (1865)
*Awake! sons of the kingdom, the King (1858)
*Awake, thou careless world, awake (1858)
*Awake, Thou spirit, who of old (1855)
*Baptized into Thy name most holy (1863)
*Be thou content, be still before (1855)
*Bed of sickness! thou art sweet (1869)
*Blessed Jesus, at Thy word (1858)
*Blessed Jesus, here we stand (1858)
*Can I my fate no more withstand (1858)
*Christ the life of all the living (1863)
*Christ the Lord is risen (1869)
*Christ the Lord is risen again (1858)
*Christ will gather in His own (1858)
*Come, brethren, let us go (1855)
*Come, Christians, praise your maker's goodness (1863)
*Come, deck our feast to-day (1855)
*Come, Holy Spirit, God and Lord (1855)
*Come, my soul, awake, 'tis morning (1855)
*Come to Thy temple here on earth (1855)
*Cometh sunshine after rain (1855)
*Comfort, comfort ye my people (1863)
*Conquering Prince and Lord of glory (1858)
*Courage my heart, press cheerly on (1869)
*Courage, my sorely tempted heart (1858)
*Dayspring of eternity! dawn on us this morning-tide (1855)
*Deal with me, God, in mercy now (1863)
*Dear Christian people, now rejoice (1869)

*Dear soul, could'st thou become a child (1855)
*Deck thyself, my soul, with gladness (1863)
*Draw us to Thee, Lord Jesus (1863)
*E'er since the day this Cross was mine (1869)
*Ere yet the dawn hath fill'd the skies (1858)
*Eternity! Eternity!--and yet (1855)
*Ever would I fain be reading (1858)
*Faith is a living power from heaven (1858)
*Fear not, O little flock, the foe (1855)
*Follow me, in me ye live (1855)
*From God shall not divide me (1863)
*From heaven above to earth I come (1855)
*From outward creatures I must flee (1869)
*From Thy heav'nly throne (1863)
*Full many a way, full many a path (1869)
*Full of wonder, full of art (1869)
*Generous love! why art thou hidden so on earth? (1869)
*Gentle Shepherd, Thou hast still'd (1858)
*Go and dig my grave today (1855)
*Go forth, my heart, and seek delight (1855)
*God, it is Thy property (1869)
*God who madest earth and heaven, Father, Son, and Holy
    Ghost (1855)
*God! Whom I as love have known (1855)
*Grant me, Eternal God, such grace (1869)
*Great High-Priest, who deigndst to be (1855)
*Hark! a voice saith, all are mortal (1863)
*Hark, the Church proclaims her honour (1863)
*Heart and heart together bound (1855)
*Heavenward doth our journey tend (1855)
*Help us, O Lord, behold we enter (1863)
*Hence my heart, with such a thought (1869)
*Here behold me, as I cast me (1858)
*Here, O my God, I cast me at Thy feet (1855)
*Him on yonder Cross I love (1858)
*Holy Ghost! my Comforter (1856)
*Holy Spirit, once again (1858)
*Hosanna to the Son of David (1855)
*How blest to all Thy followers, Lord, the road (1855)
*How brightly beams the Morning Star! (1863)
*I am baptized into Thy name, most holy (1863)
*I know a flower so sweet and fair (1863)
*I know in whom I put my trust (1858)
*I know my end must surely come (1858)
*I know, my God, and I rejoice (1863)
*I know the doom that must befall me (1863)
*I leave Him not, who came to save (1869)
*I praise Thee, O my God and Father (1863)

*I say to all men, far and near (1858)
*I who so oft in deep distress (1858)
*I will fall asleep and Jesus' arms (1869)
*I will not let Thee go, Thou help in time of need (1855)
*I will return unto the Lord (1869)
*I would I were at last at home (1869)
*If God be on my side (1855)
*If God were not upon our side (1869)
*If thou but suffer God to guide thee (1863)
*In God, my faithful God (1863)
*In life's fair Spring (1869)
*In our sails all soft and sweetly (1858)
*In peace and joy I now depart (1863)
*In the midst of life behold (1855)
*In Thee is gladness (1858)
*In Thee, Lord, have I put my trust (1863)
*Is Thy heart athirst to know (1858)
*I've ventured it of purpose free (1869)
*Jehovah, let me now adore Thee (1863)
*Jerusalem, thou city fair and high (1858)
*Jesu, be ne'er forgot (1869)
*Jesu, day by day (1863)
*Jesu, my boast, my light, my joy (1863)
*Jesu, priceless treasure (1863)
*Jesu, victor over sin (1869)
*Jesu, who didst stoop to prove (1869)
*Jesus Christ, my sure defence (1863)
*Jesus, my only God and Lord (1863)
*Jesus, my Redeemer lives (1855)
*Jesus, pitying Saviour, hear me (1858)
*Jesus, whom Thy church doth own (1858)
*Lamp within me! brightly burn and glow (1869)
*Leave all to God (1855)
*Leave God to order all thy ways (1855)
*Let nothing make thee sad or fretful (1869)
*Let the earth now praise the Lord (1863)
*Let us all with gladsome voice (1863)
*Let who will in Thee rejoice (1855)
*Lift up your heads, ye mighty gates (1855)
*Light of light, enlighten me (1858)
*Light of the Gentile nations (1863)
*Light of the Gentile world (1855)
*Lo, heaven and earth, and sea and air (1858)
*Long in the spirit world my soul had sought (1855)
*Lord, a whole long day of pain (1858)
*Lord, all my heart is fixed on Thee (1858)
*Lord God, now open wide Thy heaven (1858)
*Lord God, we worship Thee (1863)

    *Lord, hear the voice of my complaint (1863)
    *Lord Jesu Christ, the Prince of Peace (1863)
    *Lord Jesu Christ, with us abide (1863)
    *Lord Jesus Christ, be present now (1863)
    *Lord Jesus Christ, in Thee above (1858)
    *Lord, Jesus Christ, my faithful Shepherd, hear (1858)
    *Lord Jesus Christ, my life, my light (1858)
    *Lord Jesus Christ we come to Thee (1863)
    *Lord Jesus, who are souls to save (1858)
    *Lord, keep us steadfast in Thy word (1863)
    *Lord, now let Thy servant (1858)
    *Lord, on earth I dwell in pain (1855)
    *Lord, on earth I dwell sad-hearted (1863)
    *Lord! Thy death and passion give (1855)
    *Lord, to Thee I make confession (1863)
    *Loving Shepherd, kind and true (1855)
    *Make me Thine own and keep me Thine (1869)
    *Many a gift did Christ impart (1855)
    *Morning star in darksome night (1869)
    *Most high and holy Trinity! (1855)
    *My cause is God's and I am still (1858)
    *My God, behold me lying (1863)
    *My God, in Thee all fulness lies (1858)
    *My God, lo, here before Thy face (1855)
    *My God, to Thee I now command (1855)
    *My heart is filled with longing (1863)
    *My inmost heart now raises (1863)
    *My Jesus, if the Seraphim (1858)
    *My joy is wholly banished (1869)
    *My joy was ne'er unmixed with care (1869)
    *My soul, now praise Thy maker (1863)
    *Not in anger, mighty God (1863)
    *Not in anger, smite us, Lord (1855)
    *Nothing fair on earth I see (1855)
    *Now all the woods are sleeping (1856)
    *Now at last I end the strife (1858)
    *Now darkness over all is spread (1858)
    *Now fain my joyous heart would sing (1858)
    *Now God be praised, and God alone (1869)
    *Now God be with us, for the night is closing (1863)
    *Now lay we calmly in the grave (1858)
    *Now let us loudly (1863)
    *Now let us pray the Holy Ghost (1869)
    *Now rest the woods again (1855)
    *Now rests her soul in Jesus' arms (1855)
    *Now take my heart and all that is in me (1858)
    *Now thank we all our God (1858)
    *Now that the sun doth shine no more (1863)

*Now warneth us the wise man's fare (1869)
*Now we must leave our Fatherland (1858)
*Now weeping at the grave we stand (1858)
*Now will I nevermore despair of Heaven (1869)
*O blessed Jesus! (1858)
*O Christ, the leader of that war-torn host (1857)
*O Christ, Thou bright and morning star (1858)
*O Cross, we hail Thy bitter reign (1855)
*O enter, Lord, Thy temple (1863)
*O Father, Son, and Holy Ghost, Thou God, dost fix the miner'
    post (1869)
*O Father-eye, that hath so truly watched (1858)
*O Father-heart, Who hast created all (1858)
*O friend of souls, how well is me (1855)
*O glorious Head, Thou livest now (1855)
*O God, I long Thy light to see (1855)
*O God, O Spirit, light of all that live (1855)
*O God, Thou faithful God (1858)
*O good beyond compare (1869)
*O Holy Ghost! Thou fire divine (1855)
*O Holy Spirit, enter in (1863)
*O how blest are ye beyond our telling (1863)
*O Jesu Christ, most good, most fair (1869)
*O King of Glory, David's son (1858)
*O Lamb of God, most stainless (1863)
*O light, who out of light wast born (1869)
*O living bread from Heaven (1858)
*O Lord, be this our vessel now (1858)
*O Lord my God, I cry to Thee (1858)
*O Love, Who formedst me to wear (1858)
*O mighty Spirit! source whence all things sprung (1858)
*O Morning Star! how fair and bright (1863)
*O my soul be glad and cheerful (1863)
*O rejoice, ye Christians, loudly (1863)
*O risen Lord! O conquering King! (1858)
*O rose! of the flowers, I ween, Thou art fairest (1869)
*O Thou essential Word (1855)
*O Thou most highest! Guardian of mankind (1858)
*O Thou, of God the Father (1863)
*O Thou, true God alone (1869)
*O watchman, will the night of sin (1855)
*O weep not, mourn not this bier (1855)
*O well for him who all things braves (1855)
*O world! behold upon the tree (1858)
*O world, I must forsake thee (1869)
*O world, I now must leave thee (1863)
*O would, my God, that I could praise Thee (1863)
*O wouldst Thou, in Thy glory, come (1858)

*O ye halls of heaven (1869)
*O ye who from earliest youth (1869)
*Of all the joys that are on earth (1869)
*Oh blest the house, whate'er befall (1863)
*Oh how could I forget Him? (1858)
*Oh would I had a thousand tongues (1855)
*On wings of faith, ye thoughts, fly hence (1855)
*Once He came in blessing (1863)
*Once more from rest I rise again (1855)
*Once more the day-light shines abroad (1858)
*One thing is needful! let me deem (1855)
*Open now thy gates of beauty (1863)
*Our dear Lord of grace hath given (1869)
*Our Father, Thou in heaven above (1863)
*Our God, our Father (1858)
*Out of the depths I cry to Thee, Lord God! (1855)
*Patience and humility (1869)
*Praise and thanks to Thee be sung (1855)
*Praise to the Lord! the Almighty, the King of creation
    (1863)
*Pure Essence! spotless Fount of light (1855)
*Redeemer of the nations come (1855)
*Rejoice, dear Christendom to-day (1869)
*Rejoice, rejoice, ye Christians (1863)
*Rise again! yes rise again wilt Thou (1869)
*Rise, follow Me! our Master saith (1863)
*Rise, my soul, to watch and pray (1863)
*Round their planets roll the moons (1869)
*Sad with longing, sick with fears (1858)
*Salvation hath come down to us (1869)
*Seeing I am Jesus' lamb (1858)
*Seems it in my anguish lone (1858)
*Shall I not sing praise to Thee (1855)
*Shall I o'er the future fret (1869)
*Since Christ is gone to heaven, His home (1858)
*Sink not yet, my soul, to slumber (1858)
*Spread, oh spread, Thou mighty Word (1858)
*Strive, when Thou art called of God (1855)
*Sweetest joy the soul can know (1858)
*Thank God it hath resounded (1858)
*Thank God, that toward eternity (1858)
*That death is at my door (1869)
*The Church of Christ that He hath hallowed here (1858)
*The day expires; my soul desires (1855)
*The day is done, and, left alone (1863)
*The gloomy winter now is o'er (1869)
*The golden morn flames up the eastern sky (1858)
*The golden sunbeams with their joyous gleams (1855)

*The happy sunshine, all is gone (1855)
*The night is come, wherein at last we rest (1858)
*The old year now hath passed away (1863)
*The precious seed of weeping (1863)
*Thee, Fount of blessing, we adore! (1858)
*Thee, O Immanuel, we praise (1855)
*Thee will I love, my strength, my tower (1863)
*Then I have conquer'd; then at last (1855)
*Then now at last the hour is come (1858)
*There went three damsels, ere break of day (1869)
*Thou art first and best (1869)
*Thou burning love, Thou holy flame (1869)
*Thou fairest child divine (1858)
*Thou fathomless abyss of love (1869)
*Thou heavenly Lord of light (1869)
*Thou holiest love, whom most I love (1855)
*Thou love may weep with breaking heart (1858)
*Thou, solemn ocean, rollest to the strand (n.d.)
*Thou virgin soul! O thou (1863)
*Thou weepest o'er, Jerusalem (1855)
*Thou who breakest every chain (1858)
*Though all to Thee were faithless (1855)
*Thou'rt mine, yes, still Thou art mine own (1858)
*Thy parent's arms now yield thee (1858)
*Thy word, O Lord, like gentle dews (1855)
*Time, thou speedest on but slowly (1855)
*To God's all-gracious heart and mind (1869)
*To-day our Lord went upon high (1858)
*Trembling, I rejoice (1869)
*True mirrour of the Godhead! perfect light (1858)
*True Shepherd, who in love most deep (1863)
*Up! yes upward to Thy gladness rise (1858)
*Wake, awake, for night is flying (1858)
*We all believe in one true God (1863)
*We believe in one true God, Father, Son, and Holy Ghost
    (1863)
*We Christians may rejoice to-day (1863)
*Welcome, Thou victor in the strife (1855)
*What had I been, if Thou wert not (1855)
*What pleases God, O pious soul (1858)
*What shall I, a sinner, do? (1863)
*What within me and without (1855)
*Whate'er my God ordains is right (1858)
*When anguish'd and perplexed (1858)
*When in the hour of utmost need (1858)
*When my last hour is close at hand (1863)
*When o'er my sins I sorrow (1863)
*When on the Cross the Saviour hung (1863)

    *When sorrow and remorse (1855)
    *When the last agony draws nigh (1855)
    *When the Lord recalls the banish'd (1858)
    *When these brief trial-days are spent (1869)
    *Whene'er again, Thou sinkest (1858)
    *Where'er I go, whate'er my task (1858)
    *Wherefore dost thou longer tarry (1858)
    *Wherefore should I grieve and pine (1858)
    *While yet the morn is breaking (1863)
    *Who are those before God's throne (1855)
    *Who keepeth not God's word, yet saith (1858)
    *Who knows how near my end may be? (1858)
    *Who puts his trust in God most just (1858)
    *Who seeks in weakness an excuse (1855)
    *Who would make the prize his own (1858)
    *Why art thou thus cast down, my heart (1858)
    *Why haltest thus, deluded heart (1855)
    *World, farewell! of thee I'm tired (1858)
    *Worthy of praise, the Master-hand (1869)
    *Wouldst thou inherit life with Christ on high? (1855)
    *Ye heavens, O haste your dews to shed (1858)
    *Ye servants of the Lord, who stand (1863)
    *Ye sons of men, in earnest (1863)
    *Yea, my spirit fain would sink (1855)
    *Yes, there remaineth yet a rest (1855)

WINTERS, Frances W. American. Baptist

    O Lord, our God, whom all through life we praise (n.d.)

WORDSWORTH, Elizabeth (b. 1840). British. Church of England

    *God is our stronghold and our stay (1903)
    Great Ruler of the nations (1903)
    O Lord our banner, God of might (1884)

YONGE, Charlotte Mary (1823-1901). British

    Into Christ's flock we are received (1841)
    Why lived I not in those blest days? (1841)

YONGE, Frances Mary Bargus (1795-1868). British

    The Child's Christian Year (1841)

    Behold a prophet,--yea, and more (1841)
    His are the cattle on the hill (1841)

Not only as a sacrifice (1841)
Put far from us, O Lord we pray (1841)
The Assyrian king in splendour came (1841)

YORK, Sarah Emily Waldo (1819–1851).   American.   Reformed
    Dutch

    I'm weary of straying, O fain would I rest (1847)

Appendices

APPENDIX I

Hymnodists Classified by Nationality

A. American

Agnew, Edith
Akerman, Lucy
Anderson, Maria
Baker, Mary
Bates, Katharine
Baxter, Lydia
Brotherton, Alice
Brown, Jeanette
Brown, Phoebe
Cain, Florence
Campbell, Etta
Carney, Julia
Cary, Alice
Cary, Phoebe
Clapp, Eliza
Clark, Bertha
Collier, Mary
Collins, Mrs. J.A.
Copenhaver, Laura
Cory, Julia
Crozier, Maria
Dana, Mary
Demarest, Mary
Drury, Miriam
Eddy, Mary
Esling, Catherine
Fagan, Frances
Follen, Elizabeth
Garriott, Jean
Gates, Ellen
Gates, Mary
Gill, Sidney
Gilman, Caroline
Gould, Hannah
Gray, Jane

Guiney, Louise
Hale, Mary
Hale, Sarah
Hall, Elvina
Hall, Jane
Hanaford, Phoebe
Hardcastle, Cary
Harkness, Georgia
Hawks, Annie
Hinsdale, Grace
Howe, Julia
Huey, Mary
Hyde, Abby
Ikeler, Carol
Johnson, Catherine
Jordan, Diane
Judson, Emily
Judson, Sarah
Kenney, Alice
Kidder, Mary
Kimball, Harriet
Kinney, Elizabeth
Larcom, Lucy
Lathbury, Mary
Leyda, Ida
Livermore, Sarah
Mace, Frances
Marcy, Elizabeth
Mason, Caroline
Maxwell, Mary
McKeever, Harriet
Miles, Elizabeth
Miller, Emily
Moore, Jessie
Munger, Harriet

Ogdon, Ina
Oglevee, Louise
Ossoli, Sarah
Owens, Priscilla
Palmer, Alice
Palmer, Phoebe
Pearce, Selina
Perkins, Emily
Phillips, Harriet
Pollard, Josephine
Prentiss, Elizabeth
Preston, Mrs. M.J.
Price, Marion
Sangster, Margaret
Scott, Elizabeth
Scudder, Eliza
Shields, Elizabeth
Sigourney, Lydia
Smith, Caroline
Smith, Elizabeth
Spaeth, Mrs. H.R.
Stockton, Martha
Stone, Mary
Stowe, Harriet
Thomson, Mary
Torrey, Mary
Turner, Nancy
Van Alstyne, Frances
Warner, Anna
Warner, Susan
Wile, Frances
Willard, Emma
Willis, Love
Winters, Frances
York, Sarah

B. *Canadian*

Clarkson, Edith   Coghill, Annie

C. *English*

Adams, Jessie	Daye, Elizabeth	Hemans, Felicia
Adams, Sarah	Deck, Mary	Hernaman, Claudia
Alderson, Eliza	DeFleury, Maria	Herschell, Esther
Armitage, Ella	Dent, Caroline	Hornblower, Jane
Auber, Harriet	Dobree, Henrietta	Howitt, Mary
Bache, Sarah	Doudney, Sarah	Hull, Amelia
Baker, Amy	Drane, Augusta	Humphreys, Jennett
Balfour, Clara	Dunn, Catherine	Ingelow, Jean
Barbauld, Anna	Dunsterville, Patty	Inglis, Catherine
Barnard, Winifred	Durand, Emily	Irons, Genevieve
Beale, Mary	Dutton, Anne	Janvrin, Alice
Bevan, Emma	Edwards, Annie	Jarvis, Mary
Black, Mary	Edwards, Matilda	Jevon, Mary
Bode, Alice	Elliott, Charlotte	Lamb, Martha
Bourdillon, Mary	Elliott, Emily	Lancaster, Mary
Brawn, Mary	Elliott, Julia	Lee, Elvira
Brontë, Anne	Felkin, Ellen	Leefe, Isabella
Brook, Frances	Flowerdew, Alice	Leeson, Jane
Browning, Elizabeth	Forsyth, Christina	Leslie, Mary
Buchanan, Violet	Fortesque, Eleanor	Livock, Jane
Burlingham, Hannah	Fox, Eleanor	Luke, Jemima
Burman, Elizabeth	Freer, Frances	Lunn, Caroline
Butler, Mary	Fry, Henrietta	Madan, Judith
Caddell, Cecelia	Fullerton, Georgiana	Manington, Alice
Campbell, Jane	Garnier, Emily	Marston, Annie
Carpenter, Mary	Gilbert, Ann	Martineau, Harriet
Chant, Laura	Glyde, Elizabeth	Massey, Lucy
Charles, Elizabeth	Godwin, Elizabeth	Masters, Mary
Chester, Henrietta	Greenaway, Ada	Matheson, Annie
Clapham, Emma	Greenstreet, Annie	Maude, Mary
Cockburn-Campbell, M.	Greenwell, Dorothy	May, Catherine
Codner, Elizabeth	Gurney, Dorothy	Mills, Elizabeth
Colquhoun, Frances	Hankey, Arabella	Milner-Barry, Ada
Conder, Joan	Harrison, Susanna	Morris, Eliza
Cook, Eliza	Hasloch, Mary	Moule, Harriot
Coote, Maude	Havergal, Frances	Mozley, Harriet
Corelli, Marie	Hawkins, Hester	Noel, Caroline
Cowper, Frances	Haycraft, Margaret	Nunn, Marianne
Cox, Frances	Head, Bessie	Opie, Amelia
Crewdson, Jane	Headlam, Margaret	Parr, Harriet
Cropper, Margaret	Hearn, Marianne	Parson, Elizabeth
Cross, Ada	Heath, Eliza	Pearce, Lydia

Pennefather, Catherine
Peters, Mary
Petre, Katherine
Popple, Maria
Proctor, Adelaide
Pyper, Mary
Reed, Edith
Reed, Eliza
Rhodes, Sarah
Richardson, Charlotte
Richter, Anne
Roberts, Katharine
Roberts, Martha
Rossetti, Christina
Rowe, Elizabeth
Saffrey, Maria
Saxby, Jane
Scott, Elizabeth
Shapcote, Emily
Shelly Martha

Shepherd, Anne
Shipton, Anna
Sidney, Mary
Skemp, Ada
Smith, Florence
Southey, Caroline
Steele, Anne
Stevenson, Isobel
Stevenson, Matilda
Stock, Sarah
Strafford, Elizabeth
Streatfeild, C.
Taylor, Clare
Taylor, Emily
Taylor, Helen
Taylor, Jane
Taylor, Rebekah
Threlfall, Jeannette
Thrupp, Dorothy
Thwaites, Clara

Tonna, Charlotte
Trestrail, Elizabeth
Villiers, Margaret
Walker, Mary
Whiting, Mary
Whitmore, Lucy
Whittemore, Hannah
Wiglesworth, Esther
Wilkinson, Kate
Williams, Helen
Williams, Sarah
Williams, Sarah J.
Wills, Ruth
Wilson, Caroline
Wilson, Jane
Winkworth, Catherine
Wordsworth, Elizabeth
Yonge, Charlotte
Yonge, Frances

D. Irish

Alexander, Cecil
Armstrong, Florence
Bancroft, Charitie
Byrne, Mary
Clare, Mary
Cobbe, Frances

Faussett, Alessie
Gilbert, Rosa
Hinkson, Katharine
Hull, Eleanor
Macalister, Edith
Pigott, Jean

Shekleton, Mary
Stevenson, Lilian
Toke, Emma
Tynan-Hinkson, Katharine
Waddell, Helen

E. Scottish

Aird, Marion
Baillie, Joanna
Bonar, Jane
Borthwick, Jane
Clephane, Anna
Clephane, Elizabeth

Cotterill, Jane
Cousin, Anne
Duncan, Mary
Ferguson, Jessie
Findlater, Sarah
Hastings, Flora

Macdonald, Mary
Mackay, Margaret
Phillips, Edna
Simpson, Jane
Wilson, Margaret

F. Welsh

Griffiths, Ann
Maurice, Jane

Mitchell, Elizabeth

Waring, Anna

APPENDIX II

Hymnodists Classified by Denominational Affiliation

A. *Anglican Evangelical*

Hankey, Arabella

B. *Baptist*

Anderson, Maria
Baker, Mary
Baxter, Lydia
Brawn, Mary
Collier, Mary
Collins, Mrs. S.A.
DeFleury, Maria
Dent, Caroline

Dutton, Anne
Flowerdew, Alice
Hawks, Annie
Hearn, Marianne
Jordan, Diane
Judson, Emily
Judson, Sarah
Leslie, Mary

Macdonald, Mary
Pearce, Selina
Saffery, Maria
Sigourney, Lydia
Skemp, Ada
Steele, Anne
Trestrail, Elizabeth
Winters, Frances

C. *Catholic*

Caddell, Cecelia
Clare, Mary
Drane, Augusta
Freer, Frances
Fullerton, Georgiana

Guiney, Louise
Heath, Eliza
Hinkson, Katharine
Kimball, Harriet
Leeson, Jane

Petre, Katherine
Proctor, Adelaide
Shapcote, Emily
Tynan-Hinkson, K.
Wilson, Jane

D. *Christian Church*

Ogdon, Ina

E. *Christian Science*

Eddy, Mary

F. *Church of England*

Alderson, Eliza	Fortesque, Eleanor	Nunn, Marianne
Auber, Harriet	Fox, Eleanor	Pearce, Lydia
Baker, Amy	Garnier, Emily	Pennefather, Cathe
Barnard, Winifred	Greenaway, Ada	Peters, Mary
Beale, Mary	Greenwell, Dorothy	Richter, Anne
Bevan, Emma	Gurney, Dorothy	Roberts, Katharine
Black, Mary	Hastings, Flora	Roberts, Martha
Bode, Alice	Havergal, Frances	Rossetti, Christin
Bourdillon, Mary	Haycraft, Margaret	Saxby, Jane
Brontë, Anne	Headlam, Margaret	Shepherd, Anne
Brook, Frances	Hemans, Felicia	Sidney, Mary
Browning, Elizabeth	Hernaman, Claudia	Smith, Florence
Buchanan, Violet	Herschell, Esther	Southey, Caroline
Butler, Mary	Humphreys, Jennett	Stevenson, Isabel
Campbell, Jane	Ingelow, Jean	Stock, Sarah
Chant, Laura	Inglis, Catherine	Streatfeild, Charl
Charles, Elizabeth	Irons, Genevieve	Taylor, Clare
Chester, Henrietta	Janvrin, Alice	Taylor, Emily
Codner, Elizabeth	Lancaster, Mary	Threlfall, Jeannet
Colquhoun, Frances	Lee, Elvira	Thwaites, Clara
Coote, Maude	Madan, Judith	Tonna, Charlotte
Cowper, Frances	Massey, Lucy	Villiers, Margaret
Cox, Frances	Maude, Mary	Walker, Mary
Cross, Ada	Maurice, Jane	Waring, Anna
Dobree, Henrietta	May, Catherine	Whiting, Mary
Dunsterville, Patty	Mills, Elizabeth	Whitmore, Lucy
Durand, Emily	Milner-Barry, Ada	Wiglesworth, Esthe
Elliott, Charlotte	Moule, Harriot	Wilkinson, Kate
Elliott, Emily	Mozley, Harriet	Winkworth, Catheri
Elliott, Julia	Noel, Caroline	Wordsworth, Elizab
Forsyth, Christina		

G. *Congregational*

Armitage, Ella	Jarvis, Mary	Rhodes, Sarah
Brown, Phoebe	Livock, Mary	Sangster, Margaret
Clapham, Emma	Luke, Jemima	Scott, Elizabeth
Conder, Joan	Matheson, Annie	Smith, Caroline
Gilbert, Ann	Munger, Harriet	Stevenson, Matilda
Harrison, Susanna	Palmer, Alice	Stowe, Harriet
Hasloch, Mary	Parson, Elizabeth	Taylor, Jane
Hinsdale, Grace	Reed, Eliza	Wills, Ruth
Hyde, Abby		

H. Disciples of Christ

Garriott, Jean

I. Dutch Reformed

Sangster, Margaret   York, Sarah

J. Episcopal

Esling, Catherine	Scudder, Eliza	Turner, Nancy
Hale, Sarah	Stone, Mary	Warner, Anna
McKeever, Harriet	Thomson, Mary	Warner, Susan
Price, Marion		

K. Evangelical Christian

Pigott, Jean

L. Independent

Glyde, Elizabeth   Rowe, Elizabeth

M. Lutheran

Copenhaver, Laura   Spaeth, Mrs. H.R.

N. Methodist

Cain, Florence	Kidder, Mary	Owens, Priscilla
Felkin, Ellen	Lathbury, Mary	Palmer, Phoebe
Hall, Elvina	Marcy, Elizabeth	Phillips, Harriet
Hardcastle, Carrie	Miller, Emily	Van Alstyne, Frances
Harkness, Georgia	Moore, Jessie	

O. Moravian

Edwards, Annie   Lamb, Martha   Taylor, Clare

P. Plymouth Brethren

Cockburn-Campbell, M. Taylor, Rebekah   Walker, Mary

Q. Presbyterian

Agnew, Edith	Dana, Mary	Mackay, Margaret
Aird, Marion	Duncan, Mary	Oglevee, Louise
Baillie, Joanna	Findlater, Sarah	Phillips, Edna
Bonar, Jane	Gray, Jane	Prentiss, Elizabet
Borthwick, Jane	Huey, Mary	Shields, Elizabeth
Clarkson, Edith	Ikeler, Carol	Simpson, Jane
Clephane, Anna	Johnson, Catherine	Stevenson, Lilian
Clephane, Elizabeth	Kenney, Alice	Waddell, Helen
Cory, Julia	Leyda, Ida	Williams, Helen
Cotterill, Jane	Macalister, Edith	Wilson, Margaret
Cousin, Anne		

R. Quaker

Adams, Jessie	Howitt, Mary	Opie, Amelia

S. Reformed Church

Gates, Mary

T. Unitarian

Adams, Sarah	Gilman, Caroline	Mason, Caroline
Akerman, Lucy	Hale, Mary	Miles, Elizabeth
Bache, Sarah	Hornblower, Jane	Ossoli, Sarah
Barbauld, Anna	Howe, Julia	Popple, Maria
Carpenter, Mary	Jevon, Mary	Scudder, Eliza
Daye, Elizabeth	Livermore, Sarah	Taylor, Emily
Fagan, Frances	Lunn, Caroline	Williams, Sarah J.
Follen, Elizabeth	Martineau, Harriet	

U. United Church of England and Ireland

Alexander, Cecil	Cobbe, Frances	Toke, Emma
Bancroft, Charitie	Faussett, Alessie	

V. Universalist

Cary, Alice	Cary, Phoebe

Hymn Collections Arranged Alphabetically

Additional Hymns (1858); Waring, Anna
As Children Worship (1936); Brown, Jeanette
At the Beautiful Gate (1892); Larcom, Lucy

Bible Class Hymn Book (n.d.); Morris, Eliza
The Brook in the Way. Original Hymns (1864); Shipton, Anna
"Burmese Hymns"; Judson, Emily

Cantica Sanctorum (1880, 1883); Leefe, Isabella
The Child's Book of Praise (1873); Hernaman, Claudia
The Child's Christian Year (1841); Yonge, Frances
Choral Book for England (1863); Winkworth, Catherine
Christian Singers of Germany (1869); Winkworth, Catherine
Christmas Carols for Children (1884, 1885); Hernaman, Claudia

The Flock at the Fountain (1845); Adams, Sarah F.
Footprints from the Holy Deed (1863); Manington, Alice

The Garden of the Lord (1881); Armitage, Ella

Heart Melodies (1864); Hull, Amelia
The Home and Empire Hymn Book (n.d.); Hawkins, Hester
The Home Hymn Book (1885); Hawkins, Hester
Hymnau ofawl i Dduw ar Oen (1806, 1808); Griffiths, Ann
A Hymn-Book for Children (n.d.); Hull, Amelia
Hymns (1866); Kimball, Harriet
Hymns adapted to the Comprehension of Young Minds (1847, 1855);
    Shepherd, Anne
Hymns and Meditations by A.L.W. (1850, 1854); Waring, Anna
Hymns and Poems for Very Little Children (1871, 1875); Villiers,
    Margaret
Hymns and Scenes of Childhood (1842); Leeson, Jane
Hymns and Songs for Festivals and Other Occasions (1876); Baker,
    Amy
Hymns and Sonnets (1897); Scudder, Eliza

Hymns and Verses on the Collects (1865); Streatfeild, Charlotte
Hymns and Versions of the Psalms (1739); Rowe, Elizabeth
Hymns by A.M.H. (1850); Hull, Amelia
Hymns by C.F. (1861); Forsyth, Christina
Hymns Descriptive and Devotional (1858); Alexander, Cecil
Hymns for a Week (1839); Elliott, Charlotte
Hymns for All Christians (1869); Cary, Phoebe, and Charles F.
    Deems
Hymns for Children (1862); Clare, Mary
Hymns for Children (1827); Hemans, Felicia
Hymns for Children on the Lord's Prayer (1835, 1856); Mozley,
    Harriet
Hymns for Infant Children (1852); Shapcote, Emily
Hymns for Infant Minds (1809, 1810, 1844, 1877); Gilbert, Ann,
    and Jane Taylor
Hymns for Infant Schools (1827); Gilbert, Ann
Hymns for Little Children (1848); Alexander, Cecil
Hymns for Sunday School Anniversaries (1827); Gilbert, Ann
Hymns for the Church Militant (1858); Warner, Anna
Hymns for the Nursery (1806); Gilbert, Ann, and Jane Taylor
Hymns for the Seven Words from the Cross (1885); Hernaman,
    Claudia
Hymns for the Young (1830, 1836); Thrupp, Dorothy
Hymns from the German (1841); Cox, Frances
Hymns from the German (1857); Dunn, Catherine
Hymns from the Land of Luther (1854, 1855, 1858, 1862); Borth-
    wick, Jane, and Sarah Findlater
Hymns in Prose for Children (1781); Barbauld, Anna
Hymns Intended To Help the Communion of Saints (1847); Peters,
    Mary
Hymns Mostly Taken from the German (1843, 1847, 1849); Fortesque
    Eleanor
Hymns of Praise to God and the Lamb (1806, 1808); Griffiths,
    Ann
Hymns of the Reformation (1845); Fry, Henrietta
Hymns on the Holy Communion (1866); Cross, Ada
Hymns on the Imitation of Christ (1871); Massey, Lucy
Hymns on the Litany (1865); Cross, Ada
Hymns on the Love of Jesus, and the Home Above (1877); Streat-
    feild, Charlotte

The Invalid's Hymn Book (1834, 1841, 1854); Elliott, Charlotte

Lays for the Little Ones (1876); Baker, Amy
Lays of Lowly Life (1861, 1868); Wills, Ruth
A Little Book of Singing Graces (1946); Brown, Jeanette
Lyra Germanica (1855, 1858); Winkworth, Catherine

Ministry of Song (1869); Havergal, Frances
Missionary Hymns for the Use of Children (1846); Taylor, Helen
Moral Songs (n.d.); Alexander, Cecil
Morning and Evening Hymns for the Week (1870); Hearn, Marianne
A Mother's Hymns for Her Children (1849, 1852); Bourdillon, Mary

Narrative Hymns for Village Schools (1853); Alexander, Cecil

Original Hymns (1849); Maxwell, Mary
Original Hymns for Sunday Schools (1812); Gilbert, Ann, and
     Jane Taylor

Paraphrases and Hymns for Congregational Singing (1853); Leeson,
     Jane
Poems on Sacred Subjects (1834); Saffery, Maria
Prayers and Hymns from the German (1812); Knight, Ellis
The Psalmes of David (1823); Sidney, Mary

Sacred Hymns from the German (1841); Cox, Frances
Scenes and Hymns of Life (1834); Hemans, Felicia
The Silver Trumpet Answered (n.d.); Hull, Amelia
Songs amidst Daily Life (n.d.); Godwin, Elizabeth
Songs for the Weary (1865); Godwin, Elizabeth
Songs in the Night (1780); Harrison, Susanna
Songs of Eternal Life (1858); Bevan, Emma
Songs of Praise for Christian Pilgrims (1859); Bevan, Emma
Songs of Salvation (1872); Grenwell, Dorothy
Songs of Sunshine (1878); Hearn, Marianne
Songs of the Unseen Hope (1900); Massey, Lucy
The Spirit of the Psalms (1829); Auber, Harriet
Stonehurst Hymn Tunes (1921); Perkins, Emily

Three Wakings, with Hymns and Songs (1859); Charles, Elizabeth
Twelve Sacred Songs for Little Singers (1870); Havergal, Frances
Twilight Musings (1857); McKeever, Harriet
Two Friends: Songs of Salvation (1874); Greenwell, Dorothy

The Voice of Christian Life in Song (1858); Charles, Elizabeth

Wayfaring Hymns, Original and Translated (1869); Warner, Anna
Whispers in the Palms. Hymns and Meditations (1855, 1857);
     Shipton, Anna
A Wreath of Carols from the Fatherland (1864); Manington, Alice

APPENDIX IV

Titles of Hymns Arranged Alphabetically

Titles preceded by an asterisk (*) are translations.

A burdened heart that bleeds and bears (1885); Rossetti, Christina
A crown of glory bright (1868); Cary, Alice
A cry as of pain (1890, 1891); Stock, Sarah
A debtor! for the love of God unbounded (1878); Stock, Sarah
*A dread hath come on me (1863); Winkworth, Catherine
A fast before a feast (1861); Wilson, Jane
A feather'd seed that lifted is (1846); Taylor, Helen
*A few more conflicts, toils, and tears (1875); Borthwick, Jane
*A few short days of trial here (1865); Burlingham, Hannah
*A few short days of trial past (1812); Knight, Ellis
*A fortress firm and steadfast rock (1864); Cox, Frances
*A gentle angel walketh (1855); Borthwick, Jane
A happy year! even such may it be (1874); Havergal, Frances
*A holy, pure, and spotless lamb (1864); Cox, Frances
*A Lamb goes forth--for all the dues (1872); Macrae, Catherine
*A Lamb goes uncomplaining forth (1858); Charles, Elizabeth
A light streams downward from the sky (1865); Hinsdale, Grace
A little boat, with snow-sail (1853); Caddell, Cecilia
A little boy in Galilee (1959); Doughfman, Betty
A little child may know (1842); Leeson, Jane
A little ship was on the sea (1840); Thrupp, Dorothy
A little talk with Jesus (1871); Greenstreet, Annie
*A little while! so spake our gracious Lord (1858); Borthwick, Jane
*A new and contrite heart create (1841); Cox, Frances
*A pilgrim and a stranger (1858); Borthwick, Jane
*A pilgrim here I wander (1858); Winkworth, Catherine
*A rough and shapeless block of iron is my heart (1873); Durand, Emily
*A ship comes sailing onwards (1869); Winkworth, Catherine
A sinner, Lord, behold I stand (1809); Taylor, Jane
*A spotless rose is blowing (1858); Winkworth, Catherine
*A stilly angel wanders (1863); Manington, Alice

*A thousand years have fleeted (1841); Cox, Frances
A virgin heart she brought to Christ (1861); Wilson, Jane
A widowed mother lost her son (1840); Thrupp, Dorothy
*Abide among us with Thy grace (1858); Winkworth, Catherine
Abide with me. Most loving counsel this (1860); Inglis, Catherine
Above the clear blue sky (1849); Bourdillon, Mary
Accepted, perfect, and complete (1870, 1871); Havergal, Frances
*Adam did, in Paradise (1864); Manington, Alice
Advent tells us Christ is near (1870); Hankey, Arabella
Again our Lent has come to us (1861); Wilson, Jane
Again the Lord of life and light (1772); Barbauld, Anna
Again the morning shines so bright (1881); Dobree, Henrietta
*Against Thee have I sinned (1863); Winkworth, Catherine
Age after age shall call Thee blessed (1859); Charles, Elizabeth
Agnes fair martyr (1866); Moultrie, Mary
*Ah, Christian! if the needy poor (1858); Findlater, Sarah
*Ah, could I but be still (1873); Durand, Emily
*Ah dearest Lord! to feel that Thou art near (1858); Winkworth,
    Catherine
*Ah God, from heav'n look down (1863); Winkworth, Catherine
*Ah God! the world has nought to please (1869); Winkworth,
    Catherine
*Ah! grieve not so, nor so lament (1854); Findlater, Sarah
*Ah! hush now your mournful complainings (1858); Charles, Eliza-
    beth
*Ah! Jesu Christ, my Lord most dear (1869); Winkworth, Catherine
*Ah! Jesus! Lord! whose faithfulness (1867); Burlingham, Hannah
*Ah Jesus, the merit (1858); Winkworth, Catherine
*Ah! Lord, how shall I meet Thee (1863); Winkworth, Catherine
*Ah! Lord one God, let them not be confounded (1869); Winkworth,
    Catherine
*Ah! the heart that has forsaken (1859); Findlater, Sarah
Ah, what can I a sinner do? (1824); Hyde, Abby
Ah, whither flee or where abide (1865); Winkworth, Catherine
*Ah wounded Head! must Thou (1855); Winkworth, Catherine
*Ah wounded Head, that bearest (1863); Winkworth, Catherine
Ah, wretched souls who strive in vain (1760); Steele, Anne
Ah, wretched, vile, ungrateful heart (1760); Steele, Anne
*Alas, dear Lord, what evil hast Thou done (1855); Winkworth,
    Catherine
*Alas, dear Lord, what law then hast Thou broken (1863); Wink-
    worth, Catherine
*Alas for my sorrow (1869); Winkworth, Catherine
*Alas! my God! my sins are great (1863); Winkworth, Catherine
Alas! what hourly dangers rise (1760); Steele, Anne
All beautiful the march of days (1912); Wile, Frances
All before us lies the way (1841); Clapp, Eliza
*All fair within those children of the light (1858); Bevan, Emma

*All glories of this earth decay (1869); Winkworth, Catherine
 All glory be to God on high (1742); Taylor, Clare
*All glory be to God on high (1863); Winkworth, Catherine
 All hail, Incarnate God (1769); Scott, Elizabeth
*All hail to Thee, my Saviour and my God (1856); Carr, Johanna
 All men are equal in their birth (1831); Martineau, Harriet
*All my heart this night rejoices (1858); Winkworth, Catherine
*All my hope is grounded surely (1863); Winkworth, Catherine
*All poor men and humble (1928); Roberts, Katharine
*All praise and thanks to God most high (1858); Winkworth,
    Catherine
 All the way my Saviour leads me (1875); Van Alstyne, Frances
*All the world's salvation, hail (1858); Charles, Elizabeth
*All things are yours! O sweet message of mercy divine (1855);
    Borthwick, Jane
 All things bright and beautiful (1848); Alexander, Cecil
*All things hang on our possessing (1858); Winkworth, Catherine
*All ye Gentile lands awake (1855); Winkworth, Catherine
*Alleluia, sweetest music (1858); Charles, Elizabeth
 Almighty Author of my frame (1760); Steele, Anne
 Almighty Father, God of love (1878); Wiglesworth, Esther
 Almighty Father, gracious Lord (1760); Steele, Anne
 Almighty God, Thy name I praise (1830); Thrupp, Dorothy
*Almighty God, Thy truth shall stand (1845); Fry, Henrietta
 Almighty God, Who dwellest high (1809); Taylor, Jane
 Alone I walked the ocean strand (1832); Gould, Hannah
 Along the mountain track of life (1855); Cary, Alice
*Am I a stranger here on earth alone (1855); Winkworth, Catherine
 Am I called? and can it be (1834); Gray, Jane
 Amazing love that stoop'd so low (1760); Steele, Anne
 Among the deepest shades of night (1810); Gilbert, Ann
 An earthly temple here we build (1866); Johnson, Catherine
 And are there countries far away (1844); Gilbert, Ann
 And can my heart aspire so high (1780); Steele, Anne
 And canst thou, sinner, slight? (1824); Hyde, Abby
 And did the holy and the just (1760); Steele, Anne
 And didst Thou hunger, then, O Lord (1865); Streatfeild,
    Charlotte
 And didst Thou love the race (1863); Ingelow, Jean
 And is it true, as I am told? (1860); Hull, Amelia
 And is the gospel peace and love? (1760); Steele, Anne
 And now, beloved Lord, Thy soul resigning (1868): Alderson,
    Eliza
*And oft I think, if e'en earth's sin-stained ground (1845);
    Carr, Johanna
 And shall we dwell together (1846); Taylor, Helen
 And will the Lord thus condescend (1760); Steele, Anne
 Angels round the throne are praising (1840); Parson, Elizabeth

Angels singing, church bells ringing (1875); Hernaman, Claudia
*Anoint us with Thy blessed love (1869); Winkworth, Catherine
 Another called, another brought (1872); Havergal, Frances
*Another day is ended (1869); Warner, Anna
 Another portion of the span (1839); Elliott, Charlotte
 Another year is dawning (1874, 1875); Havergal, Frances
*Another year we now have enter'd (1866); Burlingham, Hannah
 Answer me, burning stars of light (1828); Hemans, Felicia
 Anywhere with Jesus (1860); Hearn, Marianne
 Are there no wounds for me? (1868, 1869); Hinsdale, Grace
*Arise, the Kingdom is at hand (n.d.); Winkworth, Catherine
 Arise, ye people, and adore (1829); Auber, Harriet
 Arm, arm, for conflict, soldiers (1880); Hernaman, Claudia
 Around a table, not a tomb (1862, 1868); Charles, Elizabeth
*Around me all is joy--and oh, my God (1859); Fry, Henrietta
 Around the throne of God in heaven thousands of children
    (c. 1838); Shepherd, Anne
 Around Thy table, Holy Lord (1842); Peters, Mary
 Art thou acquainted, O my soul? (1834); Elliott, Charlotte
*As a bird on meadows fair (1858); Winkworth, Catherine
 As Abel brought the lamb to Thee (1884); Mitchell, Elizabeth
*As each happy Christmas (1885); Spaeth, Mrs. H.R.
*As God doth lead one, will I go (1866); Burlingham, Hannah
*As God leads me, I will go (1858); Warner, Anna
 As Hebrew children strewed their plains (1881); Mitchell,
    Elizabeth
 As Mary sat at Jesus' feet (1809); Gilbert, Ann
 As on a vast eternal shore (1869); Prentiss, Elizabeth
 As once the Saviour took His seat (1824); Brown, Phoebe
*As rain and snow on earth bestow (1853); Leeson, Jane
 As Saint Joseph lay asleep (1878); Hernaman, Claudia
 As the new moons of old were given (1869); Elliott, Charlotte
*As Thou wilt, my God! I ever say (1858); Borthwick, Jane
 As Thy chosen people, Lord (1829); Auber, Harriet
 As Thy day Thy strength shall be (1859, 1867); Havergal, Frances
*As truly as I live, God saith (1865); Burlingham, Hannah
 Asleep in Jesus! blessed steed (1832); Mackay, Margaret
 Assembled at Thine altar, Lord (1836); Brown, Phoebe
*At dead of night sleep took her flight (1865); Winkworth,
    Catherine
*At eve appears the Morning star (1843); Fortesque, Eleanor
 At eventide was light (1861); Wilson, Jane
*At last, all shall be well with those His own (1858); Borthwick,
    Jane
*At length the longed-for joy is given (1858); Charles, Elizabeth
 At the font, O loving Saviour (1897); Greenaway, Ada
 At the name of Jesus (1870); Noel, Caroline
 At times on Tabor's height (1866); Kimball, Harriet
*Awake! awake! from careless ease (1843); Fortesque, Eleanor

Awake, awake, the sacred song (1760); Steele, Anne
*Awake! awake! the watchman calls (1845); Fry, Henrietta
Awake, my soul, awake my tongue (1760); Steele, Anne
Awake, my soul, lift up thine eyes (1772); Barbauld, Anna
Awake, our drowsy souls (1769); Scott, Elizabeth
*Awake! sons of the kingdom, the King (1858); Winkworth, Catherine
*Awake, thou careless world, awake (1858); Winkworth, Catherine
*Awake, Thou spirit, who of old (1855); Winkworth, Catherine

*Baptized into Thy name most holy (1863); Winkworth, Catherine
*Be not dismay'd, Thou little flock (1858); Charles, Elizabeth
Be not dismayed whate'er betide (1905); Martin, Civilla
Be our joyful song today (n.d.); Pearce, Selina
Be present, Holy Father, to bless our work today (1880, 1881);
     Roberts, Martha
*Be still my soul! the Lord is on thy side (1855); Borthwick,
     Jane
Be the living God my friend (1755); Masters, Mary
*Be thou content, be still before (1855); Winkworth, Catherine
*Be thou faithful to the end (1858); Warner, Anna
*Be thou my friend, and look upon my heart (1858); Findlater,
     Sarah
*Be Thou my vision, O Lord of my heart (1905); Byrne, Mary
*Be Thou my vision, O Lord of my heart (1912); Hull, Eleanor
Be with me in the valley (1840, 1844); Glyde, Elizabeth
Be with us all for ever more (1867); Faussett, Alessie
*Bear Jesus Christ the Lord in mind (1863); Cox, Frances
Beautiful mansions, home of the blest (1867); Van Alstyne,
     Frances
Because God loves all people (1959); Clarke, Sara
Because I know not when my life was good (1868); Williams,
     Sarah
*Because I see red tints adorning (1863); Manington, Alice
*Bed of sickness! thou art sweet (1869); Winkworth, Catherine
Before the throne of God above (1863); Bancroft, Charitie
Before the throne of God above (1862); Clare, Mary
Begin at once! in the pleasant days (1876); Havergal, Frances
Begone, my worldly cares, away (1780); Harrison, Susanna
*Behold, a Lamb! so tired and faint (1871); Carr, Mrs. E.J.
Behold a prophet,--yea, and more (1841); Yonge, Frances
Behold, according to Thy word (1853); Leeson, Jane
Behold, behold He cometh (1873); Hernaman, Claudia
*Behold how sweet it is to see (1843); Fortesque, Eleanor
*Behold me here, in grief draw near (1854); Findlater, Sarah
Behold she comes, in silence (n.d.); Wilson, Jane
*Behold that bright, that hallowed ray (1845); Fry, Henrietta
*Behold the Father's love (1859); Fry, Henrietta
Behold the glorious dawning bright (1824); Hyde, Abby

Behold the handmaid of the Lord (1864); Petre, Katherine
Behold the lilies of the field (1853); Caddell, Cecilia
Behold the loving Son of God (1742); Taylor, Clare
*Behold! Thy goodness, oh my God (1845); Fry, Henrietta
Behold, where breathing love divine (1772); Barbauld, Anna
*Bells are ringing, birds are singing (1869); Klingemann, Sophie
*Beloved and honoured, fare thee well (1858); Borthwick, Jane
Beneath the Cross of Jesus (1872); Clephane, Elizabeth
Beneath the starry arch (1841); Martineau, Harriet
Beyond the dark river of death (n.d.); Miller, Emily
Beyond the far horizon (1891); Chant, Laura
Beyond the wicked city walls (1859); Alexander, Cecil
Bless the Lord forever (1896); Haycraft, Margaret
Blessed are the children (1868); Miller, Emily
Blessed Bible! how I love thee (n.d.); Palmer, Phoebe
*Blessed Jesus, at Thy word (1858); Winkworth, Catherine
*Blessed Jesus, here we stand (1858); Winkworth, Catherine
*Blessed Jesus, we are here (1863); Manington, Alice
Blessed Jesus, wilt Thou hear us (1849); Bourdillon, Mary
Blessed Lord, our hearts are parting (1842); Peters, Mary
Blessed Saviour, I would praise Thee (1873); Taylor, Rebekah
Blest be the Lord, our strength and shield (1760); Steele, Anne
Blest Comforter divine (1824); Sigourney, Lydia
Blest Christmas morn (n.d.); Eddy, Mary
*Blest Spirit, by whose heavenly dew (1843); Fortesque, Eleanor
Bow, angels, from your glorious state (1868); Cary, Alice
Bow down, my soul, for He hath bound (1864); Petre, Katherine
Break thou the bread of life (1880, 1884); Lathbury, Mary
Breaks the joyful Easter dawn (1885); Larcom, Lucy
*Breezes of spring, all earth to life awaking (1862); Borthwick,
    Jane
Bright scenes of bliss, unclouded skies (1760); Steele, Anne
Bright was the guiding star that led (1829); Auber, Harriet
Brighten the corner where you are (1912); Ogdon, Ina
*Brightness of eternal day (1866); Burlingham, Hannah
Brood o'er us with Thy sheltering (n.d.); Eddy, Mary
Brothers, sisters, pray for us (1896); Elliott, Emily
Brothers, tread the holy portals (n.d.); Streatfeild, Charlotte

Call them in, the poor, the wretched (1862); Shipton, Anna
Called to Thy service, Lord (1889); Stock, Geraldine
Calling, calling, ever calling (1878); Hernaman, Claudia
Calm on the bosom of Thy God (1823); Hemans, Felicia
Calms the saint's slumber (n.d.); Wilson, Jane
Can guilty man indeed believe (1829); Auber, Harriet
*Can I my fate no more withstand (1858); Winkworth, Catherine
*Can you tell the countless number (1869); Klingemann, Sophie
Carry your Cross with a smile (n.d.); Ogdon, Ina

Cast thou thy care upon the Lord (1896); Moule, Harriot
Cast thy bread upon the waters (1884); Hanaford, Phoebe
Cast thy net again, my brother (1873); Baxter, Lydia
Certainly I will be with Thee (1871); Havergal, Frances
Child, amidst the flowers as play (1828); Hemans, Felicia
Child in the manger, infant of Mary (n.d.); Macdonald, Mary
*Children rejoice, for God is come (1857); Dunn, Catherine
Choose ye His Cross to bear (1829); Sigourney, Lydia
Christ has ascended up again (1853); Alexander, Cecil
*Christ, my Lord, is all my hope (1864); Borthwick, Jane
*Christ the Author of our peace (1866); Burlingham, Hannah
*Christ the life of all the living (1863); Winkworth, Catherine
*Christ the Lord, in death-bonds lay (1858); Warner, Anna
*Christ the Lord is risen (1869); Winkworth, Catherine
*Christ the Lord is risen again (1858); Winkworth, Catherine
*Christ the Lord is risen today (1853); Leeson, Jane
Christ the Lord is risen today (1869); Van Alstyne, Frances
Christ, we children sing to Thee (1881); Hearn, Marianne
*Christ, Who art both our light and day (1858); Charles,
    Elizabeth
*Christ will gather in His own (1858); Winkworth, Catherine
Christian children must be holy (1853); Alexander, Cecil
Christian, seek not repose (1839); Elliott, Charlotte
Christian, work for Jesus (1887); Hasloch, Mary
*Christ's path was sad and lowly (1858); Findlater, Sarah
Christ's soldier, rise (1860); Fullerton, Georgiana
*Church bells ring (1885); Spaeth, Mrs. H.R.
Church of God, beloved and chosen (1873); Havergal, Frances
*Clothe me, Oh Lord, with strength (1859); Fry, Henrietta
Clothe me with Thy saving grace (1867); Howitt, Mary
Clothed in majesty sublime (1840); Baillie, Joanna
Clouds and darkness round about Thee (1841); Elliott, Charlotte
*Come and let us Christ revere now (1864); Manington, Alice
Come and rejoice with me (1846, 1859); Charles, Elizabeth
*Come at the morning hour (1862); Borthwick, Jane
*Come, brethren, let us go (1855); Winkworth, Catherine
*Come brothers, let us onward (1854); Findlater, Sarah
Come, children, lift your voices (1878); Hernaman, Claudia
*Come, children! on; this way (1858); Warner, Anna
*Come, Christians, praise your Maker's goodness (1863); Wink-
    worth, Catherine
*Come, deck our feast to-day (1855); Winkworth, Catherine
*Come, enter Thine own portal (1864); Cox, Frances
*Come forth! Come on, with solemn song (1855); Borthwick, Jane
*Come forth, my heart, and seek delight (1841); Cox, Frances
Come, gentle daughters of our land (n.d.); Balfour, Clara
*Come God, Creator, Holy Ghost (1863); Manington, Alice
Come, happy children, come and raise (1830); Thrupp, Dorothy

Come, heavenly love, inspire my song (1760); Steele, Anne
Come, Holy Spirit, come, O hear an infant's prayer (1838);
    Thrupp, Dorothy
*Come, Holy Spirit, God and Lord (1855); Winkworth, Catherine
Come home, come home, you are weary of heart (n.d.); Gates,
    Ellen
Come, labour on (1859); Borthwick, Jane
*Come, let us all with one accord (1872); Chester, Henrietta
Come, Lord, and warm each languid heart (1760); Steele, Anne
Come, my fond, fluttering heart (1812); Taylor, Jane
*Come, my soul, awake, 'tis morning (1855); Winkworth, Catherine
Come, O come with thy broken heart (1875); Van Alstyne, Frances
*Come, O Thou holy dove (1857); Bunn, Catherine
Come, said Jesus' sacred voice (1792); Barbauld, Anna
Come softly, walk gently to see what is there (1937); Deming,
    Mary
*Come, Thou Creator God (1845); Fry, Henrietta
Come, Thou desire of all Thy saints (1760); Steele, Anne
Come to me, dreams of heaven (1834); Hemans, Felicia
Come to the house of prayer (1818); Taylor, Emily
Come to the land of peace (1839); Hemans, Felicia
Come to the manger in Bethlehem (1881); Mitchell, Elizabeth
*Come to Thy temple here on earth (1855); Winkworth, Catherine
*Come, tune your hearts (1841); Cox, Frances
Come unto me and rest (1858); Morris, Eliza
Come unto me, when shadows darkly gather (1839); Esling,
    Catherine
Come weary souls, with sin distressed (1760); Steele, Anne
Come, ye children, sweetly sing (1864); Campbell, Etta
Come ye yourselves apart and rest awhile (1882); Whiting, Mary
*Cometh sunshine after rain (1855); Winkworth, Catherine
*Comfort comfort ye my people (1863); Winkworth, Catherine
*Commit thou every sorrow, And care (1864); Borthwick, Jane
*Commit thy way to God (1858); Charles, Elizabeth
*Commit thy ways, thy sorrows (1845); Carr, Johanna
*Conquering Prince and Lord of glory (1858); Winkworth, Catherine
Consider the lilies, how stately they grow (1905); Brotherton,
    Alice
*Courage my heart, press cheerly on (1869); Winkworth, Catherine
*Courage, my sorely tempted heart (1858); Winkworth, Catherine
Creator God, whose glory is Creation (1970); Kenney, Alice
Creator Spirit! Thou the first (1841); Adams, Sarah

Dare we indulge to wrath and strife (1740); Scott, Elizabeth
Dark is the night, and cold the wind is blowing (1868); Van
    Alstyne, Frances
*Dark, mighty ocean, rolling to our feet (1858); Borthwick, Jane
*Darkness reigns--the hum of life's commotion (1854); Borthwick,
    Jane

Darkness shrouded Calvary (1841); Adams, Sarah
Day and night the blessings fall (1880); Lunn, Caroline
Day is dying in the west (1880, 1884); Lathbury, Mary
Day of God, thou blessed day (1841); Gould, Hannah
*Dayspring of eternity! dawn on us this morning-tide (1855);
     Winkworth, Catherine
Dead is thy daughter; trouble not the Master (1865); Alexander,
     Cecil
*Deal with me, God, in mercy now (1863); Winkworth, Catherine
*Dear Christian people, all rejoice (1858); Charles, Elizabeth
*Dear Christian people, now rejoice (1869); Winkworth, Catherine
Dear Father, hear my prayer to Thee (1959); Doughfman, Betty
Dear God of all creation (1975); Hardcastle, Carrie
Dear God, our Father, at Thy knee confessing (1928); Bates,
     Katharine
Dear Lord, on this Thy servant's day (1875); Alexander, Cecil
*Dear Lord, to hear Thee and Thy word (1873); Smith, Mrs. L.C.
Dear Lord, to Thee alone (1866); Kimball, Harriet
Dear Master, what can children do? (1882); Matheson, Annie
Dear refuge of my weary soul (1760); Steele, Anne
Dear Saint, who on Thy natal day (1853); Caddell, Cecelia
*Dear Saviour, for me hast borne (1857); Dunn, Catherine
Dear Saviour, if these lambs should stray (1824); Hyde, Abby
Dear Saviour of a dying world (1854); Waring, Anna
Dear Saviour, to Thy little lambs (1842); Leeson, Jane
Dear Saviour, when my thoughts recall (1780); Steele, Anne
*Dear soul, could'st thou become a child (1855); Winkworth,
     Catherine
*Dear to Thee, O Lord, and precious (1875); Borthwick, Jane
Death has been here, and borne away (1816); Taylor, Jane
*Deck thyself, my soul, with gladness (1863); Winkworth, Catherine
Deep thoughts were in her breast (1861); Wilson, Jane
Delightful is the task to sing (1829); Auber, Harriet
*Depart, my child (1854); Borthwick, Jane
Dim eyes for ever closed (1872); Clephane, Elizabeth
Do no sinful action (1848); Alexander, Cecil
Down in the pleasant pastures (1855); Shipton, Anna
Draw nigh unto my soul (1834); Noel, Caroline
Draw Thou, my soul, O Christ (1892); Larcom, Lucy
Draw to the Cross which Thou hast blessed (1880); Irons,
     Genevieve
*Draw us, Saviour, then will we (1857); Dunn, Catherine
*Draw us to Thee, Lord Jesus (1863); Winkworth, Catherine
Dry your tears, ye silent mourners (1864); Petre, Katherine

Early with the blush of dawn (1879); Hernaman, Claudia
Earth! guard what here we lay in holy trust (1839); Hemans,
     Felicia
*Earth has nothing bright for me (1863); Manington, Alice

*Earth has nothing sweet or fair (1841); Cox, Frances
 Earth, with its dark and dreadful ills (1870); Cary, Alice
 Earth's firmest ties will perish (1847); Peters, Mary
 Easter flowers are blooming bright (1875); Nicholson, Mary
*E'er since the day this Cross was mine (1869); Winkworth,
      Catherine
*Encumber'd heart! lay by thy sorrow (1841); Cox, Frances
 Enquire, my soul, enquire (1847); Peters, Mary
 Enter Thy temple, glorious King (1861); Miller, Emily
 Ere mountains reared their forms sublime (1829); Auber, Harriet
*Ere yet the dawn hath fill'd the skies (1858); Winkworth,
      Catherine
 Eternal Spirit, 'twas Thy breath (1740); Scott, Elizabeth
*Eternity! Eternity!--and yet (1855); Winkworth, Catherine
*Eternity! Eternity!--yet onward (1841); Cox, Frances
*Eternity! that word, that joyful word (1845); Fry, Henrietta
 Even me, even me (n.d.); Codner, Elizabeth
 Ever patient, gentle, meek (1834); Elliott, Charlotte
*Ever would I fain be reading (1858); Winkworth, Catherine
 Every morning the red sun (1848); Alexander, Cecil
*Every year that endeth (1869); Klingemann, Sophie
 Except the Lord the temple built (1875, 1881); Armitage, Ella
 External love, whose law doth sway (1879, 1881); Armitage, Ella

 Fain, O my babe, I'd have thee know (1844); Saffery, Maria
*Fairest Lord Jesus (1924); Stevenson, Lilian
*Faith is a living power from heaven (1858); Winkworth, Catherine
 Faith is a precious grace (1734, 1833); Dutton, Anne
 Faithful Shepherd, hear our cry (1878); Hernaman, Claudia
 Faithful Shepherd, of Thine own (1878); Hernaman, Claudia
 Far above the lofty sky (1858); Parson, Elizabeth
 Far from those narrow scenes of night (1760); Steele, Anne
 Father! abide with us (1860); Hearn, Marianne
 Father above, I pray to Thee (1860); Cook, Eliza
 Father, again in Jesus' name we meet (1824); Whitmore, Lucy
 Father, direct my ways (1846); Miles, Elizabeth
*Father! from Thee my greatful heart (1812); Knight, Ellis
 Father, hear as we pray (1914); Macalister, Edith
 Father, hear the prayer I offer (1859); Willis, Love
 Father, here Thy glory praising (1849); Carpenter, Mary
 Father, I know that all my life (1850); Waring, Anna
 Father, I love Thy house of prayer (1842); Leeson, Jane
 Father, if that gracious name (1835); Elliott, Julia
 Father, into Thy loving hands (1849); Saxby, Jane
 Father, let thy benediction (1844); Shelly, Martha
 Father, look upon Thy children (1878); Wiglesworth, Esther
 Father, my cup is full (1855); Shipton, Anna
 Father, my spirit owns (1842); Gilbert, Ann

Father of all, again we meet (1885); Hawkins, Hester
Father of lights, in whom there is no shadow (n.d.); Thoburn,
    Helen
Father of mercies, in Thy word (1760); Steele, Anne
Father of spirits, nature's God (1829); Auber, Harriet
Father of spirits, we entreat (1858); Parson, Elizabeth
Father! that in the olive shade (1827); Hemans, Felicia
Father, the little offering take (1846); Taylor, Helen
Father, we thank Thee for the night (1885); Weston, Rebecca
Father, when Thy child is dying (1835); Elliott, Charlotte
Father, while the shadows fall (1868); Miller, Emily
Father, who art alone (1885); Jones, Edith
Father, Who art on high (1834); Hemans, Felicia
Father, who givest us now the new year (1878); Hearn, Marianne
*Fear not, O little flock, the foe (1855); Winkworth, Catherine
 Fear was within the tossing bark (1827); Hemans, Felicia
 Fiercely came the tempest sweeping (1841); Dana, Mary
 Flee as a bird to your mountain (1841); Dana, Mary
*Flow my tears, flow still faster (1855); Findlater, Sarah
*Flowers that in Jesu's garden have a place (1853); Dunn, Catherine
*Follow me, in me ye live (1855); Winkworth, Catherine
 For a winter world of white (1959); Clarke, Sara
 For all Thy care we bless (1871); Doudney, Sarah
 For all Thy gifts of love our thanks we give (1949); Fritz,
    Dorothy
 For all Thy saints, a noble throng (1875); Alexander, Cecil
 For ever shall my fainting soul (1740); Scott, Elizabeth
 For the dear ones parted from us (1904); Greenaway, Ada
 For this new morning with its light (1959); Lee, Dorothy
 For Thy gift, the God of Spirit (1964); Clarkson, Edith
 For what shall I praise Thee (n.d.); Wilson, Caroline
 Forgive, blest shade, the tributary tear (1760); Steele, Anne
 Forgive them, O my Father (1875); Alexander, Cecil
*Forsake me not! O Thou, my Lord, my light (1883); Morgan,
    Mrs. J.P.
 Forsaken once and thrice denied (1875); Alexander, Cecil
*Fountain of all salvation, we adore Thee (1873); Durand,
    Emily
 Fountain of mercy, God of love (1803); Flowerdew, Alice
*From all created things (1873); Durand, Emily
 From all the dark places of earth's needy races (n.d.); Slade, Mary
*From blest, unconscious sleep I wake again (1864); Cox, Frances
 From glory unto glory (1873); Havergal, Frances
*From God shall not divide me (1863); Havergal, Frances
*From heaven above to earth I come (1855); Winkworth, Catherine
*From heaven angel hosts did fly (1864); Manington, Alice
*From Heaven comes the mighty Lord (1843); Fortesque, Eleanor
*From His heaven above (1869); Klingemann, Sophie
 From my dwelling midst the dead (1873); Clephane, Elizabeth
 From my everlasting portion (1874); Van Alstyne, Frances

*From out my woe I cry to Thee (1863); Manington, Alice
 From out of the clouds of amber light (1875); Alexander, Cecil
*From outward creatures must I flee (1869); Winkworth, Catherine
 From past regret and present feebleness (1871); Scudder, Eliza
*From Thy glorious heaven (1859); Bevan, Emma
*From Thy heav'nly throne (1863); Winkworth, Catherine
*From yon ethereal heavens (1845); Fry, Henrietta
 Full consecration! heart and spirit yielded (1902); Elliott,
     Emily
*Full many a way, full many a path (1869); Winkworth, Catherine
*Full of wonder, full of art (1869); Winkworth, Catherine
*Full of wonder, full of skill (1856); Carr, Johanna

*Generous love! why art thou hidden so on earth? (1869); Wink-
     worth, Catherine
 Gentle Jesus, hear our prayer (1937); Ferguson, Jessie
*Gentle Shepherd, Thou hast still'd (1858); Winkworth, Catherine
 Gently fall the dews of eve (1841); Adams, Sarah
*Give glory to the Son of God (1858); Bevan, Emma
 Give me, O Lord, a heart of grace (1905); Gilbert, Rosa
 Give me the lowest place (1866); Rossetti, Christina
 Give praise to God who made the day (1959); Ballard, Dorothy
*Give thanks for all things, children of your God (1875); Borth-
     wick, Jane
 Give to the Lord thy heart (1864); Crewdson, Jane
 Give us a dream to share (1970); Drury, Miriam
*Give us Thy blessed peace, God of all might (1862); Findlater,
     Sarah
 Glad welcome to the morning (1959); Ballard, Dorothy
*Glorious are the fields of heaven (1859); Bevan, Emma
 Glorious was that primal light (1835); Elliott, Charlotte
 Glory to God and peace on earth (1844); Livermore, Sarah
 Glory to God, for the day-spring is dawning (1861); Maurice,
     Jane
*Glory to God upon His throne (1883); Spaeth, Mrs. H.R.
 Glory to Jesus, glory (1847); Shepherd, Anne
 Glory to our great Creator (1805); Lamb, Martha
 Glory to Thee! O Lord, Who from this world of sin (1851, 1852);
     Toke, Emma
*Go and dig my grave today (1855); Winkworth, Catherine
*Go! and let my grave be made (1841); Cox, Frances
 Go and sow beside all waters (1868); Cary, Phoebe
 Go and watch the autumn leaves (1841); Adams, Sarah
*Go forth, my heart, and seek delight (1855); Winkworth, Catherine
 Go forth, my heart, and seek the bliss (1854); Follen, Elizabeth
*Go forth, Thou mighty words of grace (1843); Fortesque, Eleanor
 Go, messenger of love, and bear (1817, 1824); Brown, Phoebe
 Go not far from me, O my strength (1854); Waring, Anna

*Go out my heart, and pleasure seek (1863); Manington, Alice
Go to Thy rest, my child (1841); Sigourney, Lydia
Go when the morning shineth (1831); Simpson, Jane
Go, work in my vineyard (1873); Baxter, Lydia
God Almighty, heareth ever (1857); Strafford, Elizabeth
God Almighty, King of nations (1872); Havergal, Frances
God bless the Church of England (1878); Hernaman, Claudia
*God calling yet!--and shall I never harken? (1855); Findlater,
    Sarah
*God cares for me; why need I sorrow (1863); Manington, Alice
God chooseth out the place (1878); Wiglesworth, Esther
God doth not bid thee wait (1868); Havergal, Frances
*God doth not leave His own (1858); Warner, Anna
God draws a cloud over each gleaming morn (1859); Cobbe, Frances
God has made the changing seasons (1959); Ballard, Dorothy
God hath said, "For ever blessed" (1849); Maxwell, Mary
*God, in whom I have my being (1873); Durand, Emily
*God is in heaven! Can He hear? (n.d.); Gilbert, Ann
*God is our rock and tower of strength (1857); Dunn, Catherine
*God is our stronghold and our stay (1903); Wordsworth, Elizabeth
God is so good that He will hear (1809); Taylor, Jane
*God is the city of our strength (1845); Fry, Henrietta
*God, it is Thy property (1869); Winkworth, Catherine
*God lives! Can I despair (1869); Warner, Anna
God loved the world of sinners lost (1871); Stockton, Martha
God loves the little child that prays (1836); Thrupp, Dorothy
God, make my life a little light (1873); Edwards, Matilda
God might have made the earth bring forth (1837); Howitt, Mary
God named love, whose Fount Thou art; Browning, Elizabeth
God of ages by whose hand (1958); Burrowes, Elizabeth
God of all nations, help us now (1875); Garriott, Jean
God of all pity and all power (1899); Fox, Eleanor
God of glory, at Thy feet (1867); Brawn, Mary
God of heaven, hear our saying (1869); Havergal, Frances
God of my life, and author of my days (1772, 1773); Barbauld,
    Anna
God of my life, Thy boundless grace (1841); Elliott, Charlotte
God of my life, to Thee belongs (1769); Scott, Elizabeth
God of pity, God of grace (1858); Morris, Eliza
God of the changing year (1818); Taylor, Emily
God of the fertile fields (1955); Harkness, Georgia
God of the loving Father (1944); McCaw, Mabel
God of the sunlight hours, how sad (1834); Saffery, Maria
God of the truth from everlasting (1970); Cain, Florence
God sets a still small voice (1878); Wiglesworth, Esther
God the Father, give us grace (1865); Rossetti, Christina
God, Thou art good, each perfumed flower (1825); Follen,
    Elizabeth

God!--What a great and awful name (1809); Taylor, Jane
God, who made the earth (1870, 1879); Rhodes, Sarah
*God who madest earth and heaven, Father, Son, and Holy Ghost
      (1855); Winkworth, Catherine
God, who touchest earth with beauty (1925); Edgar, Mary
*God! Whom as I love have known (1855); Winkworth, Catherine
God will take care of you, all through the day (1881); Havergal,
      Frances
God's people all around the world (1959); Fritz, Dorothy
God's reiterated all (1873); Havergal, Frances
*Good and pleasant 'tis to see (1841); Cox, Frances
Good Daniel would not cease to pray (1812); Gilbert, Ann
Good Joseph had a garden (1926); Milner-Barry, Alda
Good news from the hills of Judea (1881); Mitchell, Elizabeth
Good news to tell (1959); Clarke, Sara
Gracious Father, we beseech Thee (1884); Hernaman, Claudia
Gracious Lord, as Thou hast bidden (1842); Reed, Eliza
Gracious Saviour, from on high (1849); Bourdillon, Mary
Gracious Saviour, gentle Shepherd (1842); Leeson, Jane
*Grant me, eternal God, such grace (1869); Winkworth, Catherine
*Grant me, O God! a tender heart (1812); Knight, Ellis
Grant the abundance of the sea (1836); Brown, Phoebe
Great Creator, who this day (1835); Elliott, Julia
Great God, and wilt Thou condescend? (1810); Gilbert, Ann
Great God, this sacred day of Thine (1760); Steele, Anne
Great God, Thy penetrating eye (1740); Scott, Elizabeth
Great God, we would to Thee make known (1834); Brown, Phoebe
Great God, wert Thou extreme to mark (1829); Auber, Harriet
*Great High-Priest, who deigndst to be (1855); Winkworth, Cather:
Great is Jehovah, King of kings (1871); Van Alstyne, Frances
Great Jehovah, King of nations (1902); Janvrin, Alice
Great Ruler of the earth and skies (1760); Steele, Anne
Great Ruler of the nations (1903); Wordsworth, Elizabeth
Great waves of plenty rolling up (1868); Cary, Phoebe
Green the hills and lovely (1904, 1905); Haycraft, Margaret
Guard well thy lips; none can know (1839); Elliott, Charlotte
Guide of my steps along life's way (1858); Clapham, Emma

Had I the wings of a dove, I would fly (1853); Aird, Marion
Hail, all hail, the joyful morn (1829); Auber, Harriet
*Hail, festal day, ever exalted (1858); Charles, Elizabeth
Hail, Holy day, most blest, most dear (1836); Elliott, Charlott
Hail! Mary, only sinless child (1853); Caddell, Cecelia
Hail the children's festal day (1875); Hearn, Marianne
Hail, thou bright and sacred morn (1835); Elliott, Julia
*Hail, Thou Head! so bruised and wounded (1858); Charles,
      Elizabeth
Hail to Thee, O Jesu (1884); Hernaman, Claudia

*Hallelujah! beauteous morning (1863); Manington, Alice
*Hallelujah! fairest morning (1858); Borthwick, Jane
*Hallelujah! I believe (1858); Borthwick, Jane
*Hallelujah! Jesus lives! (1862); Borthwick, Jane
*Hallelujah! Jesus lives! (1858); Warner, Anna
 Hallelujah! Praise the Lord (1864); Trestrail, Elizabeth
 Hallelujah, we are hastening (1847); Peters, Mary
 Hand in hand with angels (1869); Larcom, Lucy
 Happy, happy Sunday (1878); Hernaman, Claudia
 Happy is the nation whose God is the Lord (1959); Bechtel, Helen
*Hark! a voice saith, all are mortal (1863); Winkworth, Catherine
 Hark the angels bright are singing (1862); Clare, Mary
 Hark, the chorus swelling (1868); Miller, Emily
*Hark, the Church proclaims her honour (1863); Winkworth,
     Catherine
 Hark the sound of joy and gladness (1842); Gilbert, Ann
 Hark! 'tis the Saviour calls (1858); Parson, Elizabeth
 Hark, 'tis the voice of gladness (n.d.); Pearce, Selina
 Hark to the solemn bell (1842); Gray, Jane
 Hasten, Lord, the glorious time (1829); Auber, Harriet
 Have Thine own way, Lord! (1902); Pollard, Adelaide
*Have thy armour on, my soul (1865); Burlingham, Hannah
 Have you counted the cost? (1848); Leeson, Jane
 Have you ever brought a penny to the missionary box (1855);
     Elliott, Emily
 Have you not a word for Jesus? (1871, 1872); Havergal, Frances
 Have you read the wondrous story? (1830); Thrupp, Dorothy
 He came, whose embassy was peace (1855); Walker, Mary
 He cometh on yon hallowed board (1865); Alexander, Cecil
 He expecteth, He expecteth! (1894); Janvrin, Alice
 He hath spoken in the darkness (1869, 1870); Havergal, Frances
 He is coming, He is coming (1858); Alexander, Cecil
 He is risen! He is risen! tell it with a joyful sound (1846);
     Alexander, Cecil
 He knelt, the Saviour knelt and prayed (1825); Hemans, Felicia
 He led them unto Bethany (1878); Hernaman, Claudia
 He lives! the great Redeemer lives (1760); Steele, Anne
 He must reign who won the right (1881); Edwards, Annie
 He scarcely felt the cruel stones (1865); Streatfeild, Charlotte
 He sendeth sun, He sendeth shower (1841); Adams, Sarah
 He shall reign o'er all the earth (n.d.); Stock, Sarah
 He smiled as He stretched out His hand (1906); Hearn, Marianne
*He, Who the living God hath chosen (1864); Borthwick, Jane
 Hear an echo of the message (1897); Greenaway, Ada
*Hear me, my friends! the hour has come (1858); Borthwick, Jane
 Hear my prayer, O heavenly Father (1856); Parr, Harriet
 Hear the angels telling (1897); Greenaway, Ada
 Hear the Father's ancient promise (1870, 1874); Havergal, Frances

Hear ye not the tramp of reapers? (1889); Stock, Sarah
*Heart and heart together bound (1855); Winkworth, Catherine
*Heaven and earth and sea and air, God's eternal (1841); Cox,
    Frances
*Heaven and ocean, earth and air (1843); Fortesque, Eleanor
*Heaven, earth, land, and sea (1863); Manington, Alice
 Heavenly Father, from Thy throne (1852); Shapcote, Emily
 Heavenly Father, Thou hast brought us (1885); Hawkins, Hester
 Heavenly Helper, friend divine (1885); Larcom, Lucy
*Heavenward doth our journey tend (1855); Winkworth, Catherine
*Heavenward may our course begin (1843); Fortesque, Eleanor
*Heavenward our pathway lies (1857); Dunn, Catherine
*Heavenward our road doth lie (1858); Warner, Anna
*Heavenward still our pathway tends (1841); Cox, Frances
 Heir of glory, thou weeping (1864); Inglis, Catherine
*Help, Jesus, help! in woe, in need (1863); Manington, Alice
*Help, Lord Jesus, let Thy blessing (1857); Dunn, Catherine
*Help us, O Lord, behold we enter (1865); Winkworth, Catherine
*Hence my heart, with such a thought (1869); Winkworth, Catherine
 Hence, vain intruding world, depart (1760); Steele, Anne
 Heralds of Christ, who bear the King's command (n.d.); Copen-
    haver, Laura
 Here am I, for Thou didst call me (1871); Villiers, Margaret
*Here am I, Lord, Thou callest me (1862); Findlater, Sarah
*Here am I, Lord, Thou callest me (1858); Warner, Anna
*Here behold me, as I cast me (1858); Winkworth, Catherine
 Here from the world we turn (1876); Van Alstyne, Frances
*Here is Immanuel! (1864); Manington, Alice
*Here is my heart! my God I give it Thee (1854); Findlater, Sarah
 Here, Lord, what at Thy table met (1826); Taylor, Emily
*Here, O my God, I cast me at Thy feet (1855); Winkworth,
    Catherine
 Here's a message of love (1847); Shepherd, Anne
 High o'er the glittering temple (1881); Streatfeild, Charlotte
*Him on yonder Cross I love (1858); Winkworth, Catherine
 Himself hath done it all (1861); Forsyth, Christina
 His are the cattle on the hill (1841); Yonge, Frances
 His are the thousand sparkling rills (1875); Alexander, Cecil
 Holy and Infinite! viewless, eternal (1872); Havergal, Frances
 Holy brethren, called and chosen (1872); Havergal, Frances
*Holy Comforter divine (1864); Borthwick, Jane
 Holy Father, heavenly King (1832); Tonna, Charlotte
 Holy Father! in Thy mercy (1889); Stevenson, Isabel
 Holy Father, we address Thee (1847); Peters, Mary
*Holy Ghost! my Comforter (1856); Winkworth, Catherine
 Holy, holy, holy is the Lord! Sing O ye people (1869); Van
    Alstyne, Frances
 Holy is the seed-time when the buried grain (1862); Headlam,
    Margaret

 Holy Jesus, we adore Thee (1873); Hernaman, Claudia
 Holy Jesus, Who didst die (1871); Villiers, Margaret
*Holy night! calmly bright (1867); Moultrie, Mary
*Holy night! peaceful night! all is dark (1863); Campbell, Jane
*Holy Spirit, gracious Lord (1845); Fry, Henrietta
*Holy Spirit, once again (1858); Winkworth, Catherine
 Holy Trinity, before Thee (n.d.); Chester, Henrietta
 Home at last on heavenly mountains (1878); Crozier, Maria
 Hope of the world (1954); Harkness, Georgia
 Hosannah! Loud hosannah, the little children sing (1873);
     Threlfall, Jeannette
 Hosannah, they were crying (1873); Hernaman, Claudia
*Hosannah to the Son of David (1855); Winkworth, Catherine
*How beauteous shines the morning star (1865); Burlingham,
     Hannah
 How beautiful is earth (1878); Wiglesworth, Esther
 How beautiful, said he of old (1864); Stowe, Harriet
 How beautiful the hills of God (1881); Streatfeild, Charlotte
*How blessed, from the bonds of sin (1854); Borthwick, Jane
 How blest are they who daily prove (1829); Auber, Harriet
 How blest the children of the Lord (1829); Auber, Harriet
 How blest the sacred tie that binds (1792); Barbauld, Anna
*How blest to all Thy followers, Lord, the road (1855); Wink-
     worth, Catherine
*How brightly beams the Morning Star! (1863); Winkworth, Catherine
*How brightly shines the morning star (1864); Borthwick, Jane
 How can there be one holy thought! (1842); Peters, Mary
 How can we serve Thee, Lord (1873); Hernaman, Claudia
 How dreadful to be turned away (1812); Taylor, Jane
 How good is the Almighty God (1848); Alexander, Cecil
 How goodly is the earth (1839); Howitt, Mary
 How high Thou art! Our songs can own; Browning, Elizabeth
*How long, O God, Thy word of life (1845); Fry, Henrietta
*How long sometimes a day appears (1809); Gilbert, Ann
*How lovely now the morning star (1864); Cox, Frances
*How many stars are shining (1859); Bevan, Emma
 How may earth and heaven unite (1807); Barbauld, Anna
 How rich the blessings, O my God (1818); Hornblower, Jane
*How shall I get there? Who will aid? (1858); Warner, Anna
 How shall I praise Thee, O my God? (1855); Shipton, Anna
 How shall we worship Thee, O Lord? (1882); Matheson, Annie
 How sweet and silent is the place (1901); Palmer, Alice
 How sweet the melting lay (1819, 1831); Brown, Phoebe
 How sweet to be allowed to pray (1818); Follen, Elizabeth
 How sweet to think that all who love (1845); Whittemore, Hannah
 How sweet upon this sacred day (1829); Follen, Elizabeth
 How sweet when we might mingle (1866, 1875); Van Alstyne, Frances
 How tenderly Thy hand is laid (1864); Crewdson, Jane

Humbly now with deep contrition (1865); Cross, Ada
Hymns of thankfulness we raise (1897); Greenaway, Ada

 I am a little soldier (1871); Villiers, Margaret
*I am baptized into Thy name, most holy (1863); Winkworth,
      Catherine
 I am frae from home (1861); Demarest, Mary
 I am Jesus' little friend (1873); Van Alstyne, Frances
 I am learning to read the Bible (1960); Duckert, Mary
 I am not skilled to understand (1873); Greenwell, Dorothy
 I am so glad that our Father in heaven (n.d.); Oakey, Emily
 I am Thine, O Lord (1875); Van Alstyne, Frances
*I am tired, and so I seek (1863); Manington, Alice
 I am trusting Thee, Lord Jesus (1874); Havergal, Frances
 I am weak and weary, Lord (1869); Matheson, Annie
 I believe in Jesus (1960); Ballard, Dorothy
 I bore with thee long weary days and nights (1862); Rossetti,
      Christina
 I bring my sins to Thee (1870); Havergal, Frances
 I cannot find Thee! still on restless pinion (1864); Scudder,
      Eliza
 I cannot plainly see the way (1868); Cary, Alice
 I cannot walk in darkness (1875); Mason, Caroline
 I care not for riches (1878); Kidder, Mary
*I come, I come! from yon celestial clime (1845); Fry, Henrietta
*I come, O Lord, and seek for Thee (1863); Manington, Alice
 I come to Thee, my Father (1885); Hawkins, Hester
 I could not do without Thee (1873); Havergal, Frances
 I do not ask, O Lord, that life may be (1862); Procter, Adelaide
 I do not doubt Thy wise and holy will (1859); Borthwick, Jane
 I faint, my soul doth faint (1842); Gilbert, Ann
 I feel the winds of God today (1907); Adams, Jessie
 I give my life for Thee (1858, 1859); Havergal, Frances
*I go from grief and sighing (1858); Bevan, Emma
*I greet Thee, who my sure Redeemer art (1869); Smith, Elizabeth
 I had a lesson to teach them (1867); Simpson, Jane
 I had drunk with lips unsated (1868); Cary, Phoebe
*I had once four lovely children (1862); Borthwick, Jane
 I have a friend so precious (1890); Lancaster, Mary
 I have had my days of blessing (1855); Findlater, Sarah
 I have read of the Saviour's love (1847); Shepherd, Anne
 I hear the Saviour say (1865); Hale, Elvina
 I hear Thee speak of the better land (1827); Hemans, Felicia
 I hoped that with the brave and strong (1846); Brontë, Anne
*I journey forth rejoicing (1854); Borthwick, Jane
 I journey through a desert and wild (1855); Walker, Mary
*I know a flower so sweet and fair (1863); Winkworth, Catherine
*I know a sweet and silent spot (1858); Findlater, Sarah
*I know in whom I put my trust (1858); Winkworth, Catherine

*I know my end must surely come (1858); Winkworth, Catherine
*I know, my God, and I rejoice (1863); Winkworth, Catherine
*I know not what I could desire (1841); Lowe, Helen
 I know that Jesus died for me (1899); Fox, Eleanor
*I know that my Redeemer lives (1863); Manington, Alice
*I know the doom that must befall me (1863); Winkworth, Catherine
*I know Thy voice, my Shepherd (1873); Durand, Emily
*I leave Him not, who came to save (1869); Winkworth, Catherine
 I like to think of Jesus (1958); Shields, Elizabeth
 I linger round the fold of God (1885); Streatfeild, Charlotte
 I love, I love my Master (1876, 1878); Havergal, Frances
 I love that Holy Scripture (n.d.); Taylor, Helen
 I love the courts of Jesus (1861); Wilson, Jane
 I love to feel that I am taught (1867, 1869); Havergal, Frances
 I love to hear the story (1867); Miller, Emily
 I love to steal awhile away (1818, 1824); Brown, Phoebe
 I love to tell the story, of unseen things above (1868, 1874);
       Hankey, Arabella
 I love to think that Jesus saw (1908); Skemp, Ada
 I need no other plea (1869); Elliott, Charlotte
 I need no prayers to saints (1869); Elliott, Charlotte
 I need Thee every hour (1872); Hawks, Annie
*I now commence to separate stage (1843); Fortesque, Eleanor
*I praise Thee, O my God and Father (1863); Winkworth, Catherine
*I rest with Thee, Lord! whither should I go (1855); Borthwick,
       Jane
 I saw Him leave his Father's throne (1868, 1879); Hankey,
       Arabella
*I say to all men, far and near (1858); Winkworth, Catherine
*I say to everyone, He lives (1844); Lowe, Helen
*I sing to Thee with mouth and heart (1864); Cox, Frances
 I stood outside the gate (1878); Pollard, Josephine
 I thank the goodness and the grace (1809); Gilbert, Ann
 I thank Thee, Lord, that Thou hast shown (1890); Marston, Annie
 I thank Thee, O my God, Who made (1858); Procter, Adelaide
 I think of Thee, O Saviour (1857); Threlfall, Jeannette
 I think when I read that sweet story of old (1841, 1853); Luke,
       Jemima
 I want a Sabbath with Thee (1864); Crewdson, Jane
 I want that adorning divine (1848); Elliott, Charlotte
 I want to be an angel (1854); Gill, Sidney
 I weep, but not rebellious tears (1826); Southey, Caroline
*I who so oft in deep distress (1858); Winkworth, Catherine
*I will fall asleep and Jesus' arms (1869); Winkworth, Catherine
 I will follow the upward road (n.d.); Edgar, Mary
*I will love Thee, all my treasure (1855); Findlater, Sarah
*I will not let Thee go, Thou help in time of need (1855);
       Winkworth, Catherine

*I will return unto the Lord (1869); Winkworth, Catherine
 I will sing you a song of that beautiful land (n.d.); Gates, Ell
 I would be Thine, O take my heart (1842); Reed, Eliza
 I would be Thy little lamb (1871); Van Alstyne, Frances
 I would believe; but my weak heart (1835); Elliott, Julia
 I would choose to be a door-keeper (n.d.); Hinkson, Katharine
 I would have gone, God bade me stay (1866); Rossetti, Christina
*I would I were lost at home (1869); Winkworth, Catherine
*If God be on my side (1855); Winkworth, Catherine
*If God were not upon our side (1845); Fry, Henrietta
*If God were not upon our side (1869); Winkworth, Catherine
 If I come to Jesus, He will make me glad (1868); Van Alstyne,
     Frances
*If I have only Him (1841); Lowe, Helen
*If I trust in God alone (1862); Rowan, Frederica
 If love, the noblest, purest, blest (1837); Taylor, Emily
*If only He is mine (1855); Borthwick, Jane
 If the world seems cold to you (1869); Larcom, Lucy
*If thou but suffer God to guide thee (1863); Winkworth, Catherin
 If washed in Jesus' blood (1870); Wilson, Margaret
 If you cannot on the ocean (1860); Gates, Ellen
 I'll bless Jehovah's glorious name (1795); Daye, Elizabeth
 I'll never forsake Thee (1860); Fullerton, Georgiana
*I'll not leave Jesus, never, never (1858); Warner, Anna
*I'll sing to Thee with heart and mouth (1863); Manington, Alice
 I'm a pilgrim, and I'm a stranger (1841); Dana, Mary
 I'm journeying through a desert world (1873); Pennefather,
     Catherine
 I'm kneeling, Lord, at mercy's gate (1879); Baxter, Lydia
 I'm weary of straying, O fain would I rest (1847); York, Sarah
 Immortal Spirit! wake, arise (1839); Elliott, Charlotte
 In Bethlehem near starlit skies (1963); Stutsman, Grace
 In breathless silence kneel (1860); Fullerton, Georgiana
 In Christ I feel the heart of God (1881); Larcom, Lucy
*In faith we sing this song of thankfulness (1858); Bevan, Emma
 In full and glad surrender (1879); Havergal, Frances
*In God, my faithful God (1863); Winkworth, Catherine
 In God's great field of labour (1867, 1869); Havergal, Frances
 In golden light of early days (1906); Haycraft, Margaret
 In heavenly love abiding (1850); Waring, Anna
*In Jesus' arms her soul doth rest (1858); Bevan, Emma
*In life's fair spring (1869); Winkworth, Catherine
*In many a form I see Thee oft (1841); Lowe, Helen
 In our hearts celestial voices softly say (1901); Corelli,
     Marie
*In our sails all soft and sweetly (1858); Winkworth, Catherine
*In peace and joy I now depart (1863); Winkworth, Catherine
 In the bleak midwinter (1872); Rossetti, Christina

In the crowds that came to Jesus (1959); Ballard, Dorothy
In the dark and silent night (1848); Leeson, Jane
In the desert all alone (1881); Mitchell, Elizabeth
In the early morning (n.d.); Leyda, Ida
In the evening there is weeping (1869, 1870); Havergal, Frances
In the fadeless spring-time (1872, 1873); Baxter, Lydia
*In the far celestial land (1872); Chester, Henrietta
*In the grey of the morning when shades pass away (1857); Dunn,
    Catherine
In the hollow of His hand (n.d.); Pearce, Lydia
*In the midst of life behold (1855); Winkworth, Catherine
In the name of God our Father (1885); Hawkins, Hester
In the paradise of Jesus (1877); Streatfeild, Charlotte
In the rich man's garden (1853); Alexander, Cecil
*In Thee is gladness (1858); Winkworth, Catherine
*In Thee, Lord, have I put my trust (1863); Winkworth, Catherine
In Thee my powers and treasures live (1855, 1864); Scudder,
    Eliza
In this world of sin and sorrow (1763); Madan, Judith
In Thy cleft, O Rock of Ages (1880); Van Alstyne, Frances
In Thy holy garden ground (1871); Doudney, Sarah
Increase our faith, beloved Lord (1878); Havergal, Frances
*Infant holy, infant lowly (1926); Reed, Edith
Into Christ's flock we are received (1841); Yonge, Charlotte
Into His summer garden (1873); Clephane, Elizabeth
*Is God for me? I fear not (1858); Bevan, Emma
Is it for me, dear Saviour? (1871, 1872); Havergal, Frances
Is the cruse of comfort wasting (1859); Charles, Elizabeth
Is there a lone and dreary hour? (1820); Gilman, Caroline
Is there one heart, dear Saviour, here (1858); Parson, Elizabeth
*Is thy heart athirst to know (1858); Winkworth, Catherine
*Is Thy work all ended, Lord? (1862); Borthwick, Jane
Israel of God, awaken (1871, 1872); Havergal, Frances
It is a day of gladness (1881); Hernaman, Claudia
It is an easy thing to say (1866); Kimball, Harriet
*It is evening, and the hour, Lord (1863); Manington, Alice
*It is finished! finished! yea (1857); Dunn, Catherine
It is finished! He hath seen (1853); Caddell, Cecelia
*It is, indeed, a precious thing (1863); Manington, Alice
It is Thanksgiving time again (1959); Lee, Dorothy
It is the Lord Himself Who fends (1881); Armitage, Ella
*It is the midnight hour (1858); Charles, Elizabeth
It shall be now (1890); Marston, Annie
It matters not what be Thy lot (n.d.); Eddy, Mary
It passeth knowledge (1863); Shekleton, Mary
It was early in the morning (1853); Alexander, Cecil
I've found joy in sorrow (1864); Crewdson, Jane
*I've ventured it of purpose free (1869); Winkworth, Catherine

Jehovah elohim! Creator great (1861); Forsyth, Christina
Jehovah, great and awful name (1829); Auber, Harriet
*Jehovah, let me now adore Thee (1863); Winkworth, Catherine
Jehovah reigns, let every nation hear (1772); Barbauld, Anna
Jehovah reigns, O earth rejoice (1829); Auber, Harriet
Jehovah's covenant shall endure (1872, 1876); Havergal, Frances
*Jerusalem! thou city builded high (1866); Burlingham, Hannah
*Jerusalem, thou city fair and high (1858); Winkworth, Catherine
*Jerusalem, thou city rear'd on high (1863); Manington, Elizabeth
*Jerusalem! thou city towering high (1864); Cox, Frances
*Jerusalem! thou glorious city-height (1858); Bevan, Emma
*Jesu, be ne'er forgot (1869); Winkworth, Catherine
Jesu, by the Lenten fast (1897); Greenaway, Ada
Jesu! by whose Almighty grace (1870); Toke, Emma
*Jesu, day by day (1863); Winkworth, Catherine
Jesu, loving Saviour (1885); Hawkins, Hester
*Jesu, my boast, my light, my joy (1863); Winkworth, Catherine
*Jesu, priceless treasure (1863); Winkworth, Catherine
*Jesu, our Redeemer, now (1858); Charles, Elizabeth
*Jesu, victor over sin (1869); Winkworth, Catherine
Jesu, we adore Thee (1878); Hernaman, Claudia
*Jesu, who didst stoop to prove (1869); Winkworth, Catherine
Jesus, a child His course began (1859); Ossoli, Sarah
Jesus! all-sufficiency (1882); Stock, Sarah
Jesus bids us shine with a pure, clear light (1868); Warner,
    Susan
Jesus, blessed Saviour (1872, 1873); Havergal, Frances
Jesus calls, He it is (1892); Stock, Sarah
Jesus calls us; o'er the tumult (1852); Alexander, Cecil
Jesus Christ is risen (1960); Ballard, Dorothy
Jesus Christ, my Lord and King (1842); Leeson, Jane
Jesus Christ, my Lord and Saviour (1810); Taylor, Jane
*Jesus Christ, my sure defence (1863); Winkworth, Catherine
*Jesus, come Thyself to me (1864); Manington, Alice
Jesus demands this heart of mine (1760); Steele, Anna
Jesus, ever present with Thy Church below (1861); Wilson, Jane
Jesus, glorious Prince of angels (1884); Mitchell, Elizabeth
Jesus, gracious One, calleth now to thee (1881); Collins,
    Mrs. S.A.
Jesus, great Redeemer (1866); Cross, Ada
*Jesus, help conquer! my spirit is sinking (1858); Warner, Anna
*Jesus, help conquer, Thou Prince of my being (1863); Manington,
    Alice
Jesus, high in glory (1847); McKeever, Harriet
Jesus, holy, undefiled (1852); Shapcote, Emily
*Jesus' hour is not yet come (1855); Borthwick, Jane
Jesus! how much Thy name unfolds (1842); Peters, Mary
Jesus, I am resting, resting (1875); Pigott, Jean

Jesus I love Thee (1873); Van Alstyne, Frances
*Jesus! I place my trust in Thee (1843); Fortesque, Eleanor
 Jesus, I will trust Thee (1855); Walker, Mary
*Jesus in bonds of death had lain (1864); Borthwick, Jane
 Jesus, in loving worship (1843); Hernaman, Claudia
*Jesus is come, O joy heaven-lighted (1858); Warner, Anna
*Jesus is the sinner's friend (1857); Dunn, Catherine
*Jesus! Jesus! come to me (1865); Burlingham, Hannah
 Jesus, keep me near the Cross (1869); Van Alstyne, Frances
*Jesus lives! no longer now (1864); Cox, Frances
 Jesus lives! with Him shall I (1869); Warner, Anna
 Jesus, Lord of heaven above (1854); Waring, Anna
*Jesus, Lord, Thy servants see (1841); Cox, Frances
 Jesus, Lord, to Thee we sing (1829); Auber, Harriet
 Jesus loves me, this I know (1859); Warner, Anna
 Jesus, Master, hear my cry (1855); Shipton, Anna
 Jesus, Master, whose I am (1865, 1869); Havergal, Frances
*Jesus, my eternal trust (1858); Charles, Elizabeth
*Jesus, my only God and Lord (1863); Winkworth, Catherine
*Jesus, my Redeemer lives (1855); Winkworth, Catherine
 Jesus, my Saviour, look on me (1869); Elliott, Charlotte
*Jesus, my Sun, before whose beams (1873); Durand, Emily
*Jesus, my Sun! before whose eye (1859); Fry, Henrietta
 Jesus, of Thee we ne'er would tire (1847); Peters, Mary
 Jesus, only! in the shadow (1870, 1871); Havergal, Frances
 Jesus, our loving friend (1959); McCollough, Betty
*Jesus, pitying Saviour, hear me (1858); Winkworth, Catherine
 Jesus, royal Jesus (1873); Hernaman, Claudia
*Jesus, Saviour, once again (1857); Dunn, Catherine
 Jesus, Saviour, pass not by (1880); Kinney, Elizabeth
 Jesus, Saviour! Thou dost know (n.d.); Dent, Caroline
*Jesus shall lead on (1846); Borthwick, Jane
*Jesus! source of life eternal (1865); Burlingham, Hannah
*Jesus, sun of righteousness (1855); Borthwick, Jane
 Jesus, tender Shepherd, hear me (1839, 1841); Duncan, Mary
 Jesus, tender Shepherd, seeking for Thine own (1885); Streat-
     feild, Charlotte
 Jesus, that condescending King (1809); Gilbert, Ann
 Jesus, the children are calling (1866); Matheson, Annie
 Jesus, the ladder of my faith (1866); Kimball, Harriet
 Jesus, the rays divine (1868, 1869); Hinsdale, Grace
 Jesus the water of life has given (1867); Van Alstyne, Frances
 Jesus, this mid-day hour (1857); Brown, Phoebe
 Jesus, Thou source divine (1760); Steele, Anne
*Jesus, Thy life is mine (1876); Havergal, Frances
*Jesus, 'tis my aim divine (1857); Dunn, Catherine
 Jesus was once a little child (1862); Clare, Mary
 Jesus was once despised and low (1809); Gilbert, Ann

Jesus, we love to meet (1858); Parson, Elizabeth
Jesus, we thank Thee for Thy day (1849); Bourdillon, Mary
Jesus, what once Thou wast (1881); Charles, Elizabeth
*Jesus! what was that which drew Thee (1855); Findlater, Sarah
Jesus, Who lived above the sky (1812); Gilbert, Ann
*Jesus, whom I long for (1873); Durand, Emily
*Jesus, Whom Thy Church doth own (1858); Winkworth, Catherine
*Jesus, with Thee I would abide (1873); Durand, Emily
Join, all ye servants of the Lord (1829); Auber, Harriet
Joined to Christ by mystic union (1871, 1872); Havergal, Frances
*Joy to the followers of the Lord (1820, 1825); Barbauld, Anna
Joy-bells ringing, children singing (1878); Pollard, Josephine
*Joyful light of holy glory (1858); Charles, Elizabeth
Just as I am, Thine own to be (1887); Hearn, Marianne
Just as I am, without one plea (1836); Elliott, Charlotte
Just when Thou wilt, O Master, call (1878); Havergal, Frances

Kind Shepherd, see Thy little lamb (1885); Hawkins, Hester
King eternal and immortal (1871, 1874); Havergal, Frances
King eternal, King immortal (1876); Cousin, Anne
King of glory, Saviour dear (1881); Mitchell, Elizabeth
King of saints and King of glory (1853); Leeson, Jane
Knocking, knocking, who is there? (1867); Stowe, Harriet

Labourers of Christ, arise (1836); Sigourney, Lydia
Lamb most holy, King most lowly (1880); Mitchell, Elizabeth
Lamb of God, who came from heaven (1849); Bourdillon, Mary
*Lamp within me! brightly burn and glow (1869); Winkworth,
     Catherine
Land of peace, and love, and brightness (1871); Doudney, Sarah
Launch thy bark, mariner (1826); Southey, Caroline
Launched upon the stormy ocean (1827); Colquhoun, Frances
Lead me to Jesus (1871); Van Alstyne, Frances
Leaning on Thee, my Guide, my Guide, my Friend (1836); Elliott,
     Charlotte
*Leave all to God (1855); Winkworth, Catherine
*Leave God to order all thy ways (1855); Winkworth, Catherine
Leave me, dear ones, to my slumber (1868); Cary, Alice
Leaves have their time to fall (1827); Hemans, Felicia
*Let love weep--it cometh (1858); Warner, Anna
Let me be with Thee where Thou art (1836); Elliott, Charlotte
*Let me go, let me go, Jesus (1867); Ashley, Mrs. E.
Let me suffer, let me drain (1867); Howitt, Mary
*Let nothing make me sad or fretful (1869); Winkworth, Catherine
Let the children come, Christ said (1877, 1881); Hearn, Marianne
*Let the earth now praise the Lord (1863); Winkworth, Catherine
Let the song go round the earth (1898, 1899); Stock, Sarah
Let there be light at eventide (1896); Haycraft, Margaret

*Let us all with gladsome voice (1863); Winkworth, Catherine
 Let us sing our song of praise (1947); Barnard, Winifred
 Let us sing with one accord (1836); Thrupp, Dorothy
*Let who will in Thee rejoice (1855); Winkworth, Catherine
 Let whoever will enquire (1855); Scudder, Eliza
 Life of our life, and light of all our seeing (1875); Scudder,
     Eliza
 Life-light waneth to an end (1874); Clephane, Elizabeth
*Life's course must recommence to-day (1841); Cox, Frances
 Lift up, lift up thy voice with singing (1878); Lathbury, Mary
*Lift up my soul to Thee, O Lord (1843); Fortesque, Eleanor
*Lift up your heads, ye mighty gates (1855); Winkworth, Catherine
 Light after darkness, gain after loss (1879); Havergal, Frances
 Light and comfort of my soul (1867); Van Alstyne, Frances
*Light of light, enlighten me (1858); Winkworth, Catherine
*Light of the Gentile nations (1863); Winkworth, Catherine
*Light of the Gentile world (1855); Winkworth, Catherine
 Light of the world, faint were our weary feet (1901, 1904);
     Chant, Laura
 Light of the world, O shine on us (1865); Cross, Ada
 Light of the world, that shines to bless (1858); Alexander, Cecil
 Light waits for us in heaven (1868); Cary, Alice
 Like a river glorious, is God's perfect peace (1879); Havergal,
     Frances
*Listen to our prayer (1956); Brown, Leila
 Little beams of rosy light (1869); Van Alstyne, Frances
 Little children, Advent bids you (1878); Wiglesworth, Esther
*Little children, God above (1858); Bevan, Emma
 Little drops of water (1845); Carney, Julia
 Little feet are passing (1866); Hearn, Marianne
 Little raindrops feed the rill (1841); Sigourney, Lydia
 Living or dying, Lord, I would be Thine (1841); Adams, Sarah
 Lo! amid the shades of night (1891); Thomson, Mary
 Lo, at noon, 'tis sudden night (1810); Gilbert, Ann
*Lo, heaven and earth and sea and air (1858); Winkworth, Catherine
*Lo! in the East the golden morn appearing (1859); Fry, Henrietta
*Long in the spirit world my soul had sought (1855); Winkworth,
     Catherine
*Lo! God to heaven ascendeth (1841); Cox, Frances
*Lo! my choice is now decided (1841); Cox, Frances
*Lo! now the victory's gain'd me (1841); Cox, Frances
*Lo, on a mount a tree doth stand (1885); Spaeth, Mrs. H.R.
*Lo! steep and thorny is the road (1843); Fortesque, Eleanor
*Lo the day of wrath, the day (1858); Charles, Elizabeth
*Lo the day, the day of life (1858); Charles, Elizabeth
*Lo! the world from slumber risen (1872); Chester, Henrietta
 Lo, to us a child is born (1873); Threlfall, Jeannette
 Lo, where a crowd of pilgrims toll (1792); Barbauld, Anna

*Long hast Thou wept and sorrowed (1862); Borthwick, Jane
*Looking from this vale of sadness (1865); Burlingham, Hannah
 Looking unto Jesus (1864); Crewdson, Jane
 Looking unto Jesus, never need we yield (1876); Havergal, Franc
 Looking upward every day (1881); Butler, Mary
 Lord, a happy child of Thine (1850); Waring, Anna
 Lord, a little band and lowly (1844); Shelly, Martha
 Lord, a little band of children (1897); Greenaway, Ada
*Lord, a whole long day of pain (1858); Winkworth, Catherine
*Lord, all my heart is fixed on Thee (1858); Winkworth, Catherin
 Lord and Master, who hast called us (1913); Smith, Florence
 Lord, at Thy mercy seat (1868); Van Alstyne, Frances
 Lord, deliver, Thou canst save (1836); Follen, Elizabeth
*Lord God, now open wide Thy heaven (1858); Winkworth, Catherine
 Lord God, the strength and stay of all (1870); Toke, Emma
*Lord God, we worship Thee (1863); Winkworth, Catherine
*Lord! grant a new-born heart to me (1843); Fortesque, Eleanor
 Lord, guard and guide the men who fly (1934); Hamilton, Mary
*Lord, hear the voice of my complaint (1863); Winkworth, Catheri
 Lord, help us as we hear (n.d.); Gilbert, Ann
 Lord, help us as we sing (1886); Shelly, Martha
 Lord, how mysterious are Thy ways (1760); Steele, Anne
 Lord, how shall wretched sinners dare (1780); Steele, Anne
 Lord, I come at last to Thee (1890); Marston, Annie
 Lord, I desire to live as one (1861); Bancroft, Charitie
 Lord, I have sinned, but pardon me (1873); Hernaman, Claudia
 Lord, I hear of showers of Blessing (1860); Codner, Elizabeth
 Lord, I know a work is waiting (1898); Janvrin, Alice
 Lord, I would own Thy tender care (1809); Taylor, Jane
 Lord, in all our trials here (1852); Toke, Emma
 Lord, in Thy great, Thy glorious Name (1760); Steele, Anne
*Lord, in Thy mercy and Thy grace (1845); Fry, Henrietta
*Lord Jesu Christ, the Prince of Peace (1863); Winkworth,
      Catherine
*Lord Jesu Christ, with us abide (1863); Winkworth, Catherine
*Lord Jesus, be Thou with us now (1914); Macalister, Edith
*Lord Jesus Christ, be present now (1863); Winkworth, Catherine
*Lord Jesus Christ, in Thee above (1858); Winkworth, Catherine
*Lord Jesus Christ, my faithful Shepherd, hear (1858); Winkworth
      Catherine
*Lord Jesus Christ, my life, my light (1858); Winkworth, Catheri
*Lord Jesus Christ we come to Thee (1863); Winkworth, Catherine
 Lord Jesus! come; for here (1831); Martineau, Harriet
 Lord Jesus, in Thy name alone (1847); Peters, Mary
*Lord Jesus, who our souls to save (1858); Winkworth, Catherine
*Lord, keep us steadfast in Thy word (1863); Winkworth, Catherin
*Lord, make my spirit still (1869); Warner, Anna
 Lord, may the spirit of this feast (1845); Sigourney, Lydia
*Lord, my house of clay (1858); Warner, Anna

Lord, my times are in Thy hand (1789); Taylor, Clare
Lord, my trust I repose on Thee (1877); Van Alstyne, Frances
*Lord, none to Thee may be compared (1866); Burlingham, Hannah
*Lord, now let Thy servant (1858); Winkworth, Catherine
 Lord of all power and might (1870); Toke, Emma
 Lord of all the ages of Eternity (1889); Janvrin, Alice
 Lord of glory, Who hast bought us (1864, 1868); Alderson,
     Eliza
 Lord of light, and Fount of love (1875); Stock, Sarah
 Lord of light and life (1870); Toke, Emma
 Lord of love, and truth, and grace (n.d.); Stock, Sarah
 Lord of might, our land's defender (1903); Whiting, Mary
 Lord of my life, O may Thy praise (1760); Steele, Anne
 Lord of the golden harvest (1871); Doudney, Sarah
 Lord of Thy mercy, hear our cry (1852); Toke, Emma
*Lord, on earth I dwell in pain (1855); Winkworth, Catherine
*Lord, on earth I dwell sad-hearted (1863); Winkworth, Catherine
*Lord our God, in reverence lowly (1858); Findlater, Sarah
 Lord, Thou didst love Jerusalem (1855); Walker, Mary
*Lord, Thou hast bid us labour, bid us toil (1858); Warner, Anna
 Lord, Thou knowest all the weakness (1862); Borthwick, Jane
 Lord, through the desert drear and wide (1847); Peters, Mary
*Lord! Thy death and passion give (1855); Winkworth, Catherine
 Lord, Thy ransomed Church is waking (1874); Stock, Sarah
*Lord, to Thee I make confession (1863); Winkworth, Catherine
 Lord, to Thee my heart ascending (1867); Codner, Elizabeth
 Lord, to Thy people and dispense (1789); Taylor, Clare
 Lord, we come to ask Thy blessing (1881); Dobree, Henrietta
 Lord, we bend before Thee now (1858); Parson, Elizabeth
 Lord, we know that Thou art near us (1864); Crewdson, Jane
 Lord, we meet to pray and praise (1858); Clapham, Emma
 Lord, we see the day approaching (1842); Peters, Mary
 Lord, what is life? 'tis like a flower (1809); Gilbert, Ann
 Lord, when we have not any light (1880); Matheson, Annie
 Lord, who throughout these forty days (1873); Hernaman, Claudia
 Lord, with a very tired mind (1879); Stone, Mary
 Loud in exultation (1861); Wilson, Jane
 Love and a Cross together blest (1862); Borthwick, Jane
 Love and death have wrestled fiercely (1861); Wilson, Jane
 Love and kindness we may measure (1809); Taylor, Jane
*Love divine! my love commanding (1865); Burlingham, Hannah
*Love doth the whole--not part--desire (1869); Warner, Anna
 Love, thou dost all excel (1864); Petre, Katherine
*Love, who in the first beginning (1864); Cox, Frances
*Loved one! who by grace hast wrought me (1862); Findlater,
     Sarah
 Lover of souls and Lord of all the living (n.d.); Waddell, Helen
 Loving Father, throned in glory (1903); Leefe, Isabella

Loving Saviour, hear my cry (1873); Van Alstyne, Frances
*Loving Shepherd, kind and true (1855); Winkworth, Catherine
*Loving Shepherd of Thy sheep (1842); Leeson, Jane
*Low at Thy feet my spirit lies (1862); Borthwick, Jane
 Lowly and solemn be Thy children's cry to Thee (1832); Hemans,
     Felicia

 Magnify the Lord today (1884); Hernaman, Claudia
 Maiden Mother, meek and mild (1853); Caddell, Cecelia
*Make me Thine own and keep me Thine (1869); Winkworth, Catherine
*Many a gift did Christ impart (1855); Winkworth, Catherine
 Many sons to glory bring (1847); Peters, Mary
 March, my little children (1885); Humphreys, Jennett
 March on, march on, ye soldiers true (1886); Armitage, Ella
 Mary, mother! shield us (1860); Fullerton, Georgiana
 Master, how shall I bless Thy name? (1875); Havergal, Frances
 Master, speak! Thy servant heareth (1867, 1869); Havergal, Franc
 Master, the tempest is raging (1874); Baker, Mary
 Master, where abidest Thou? (1859); Charles, Elizabeth
 May the mind of Christ my Saviour (1912); Wilkinson, Kate
 'Midst the bitter waters Moses (1861); Wilson, Jane
 Mine be the tongue that always shrinks (1875); Fagan, Frances
 Mine eyes have seen the glory of the coming of the Lord (1861,
     1862); Howe, Julia
 More about Jesus would I know (1887); Hewitt, Eliza
 More love to Thee, O Christ (1869, 1872); Prentiss, Elizabeth
*Morning glance of verity (1863); Manington, Alice
 Morning has broken like the first morn (1931); Farjeon, Eleanor
*Morning star in darksome night (1869); Winkworth, Catherine
*Mortals who have God offended (1841); Cox, Frances
*Most high and holy Trinity! (1855); Winkworth, Catherine
*Most high and holy Trinity, Thou God (1841); Cox, Frances
*Most holy God! to Thee I cry (1843); Fortesque, Eleanor
 Mourner, whereso'er thou art (1871, 1873); Van Alstyne, Frances
*My cause is God's and I am still (1858); Winkworth, Catherine
 My Father, I thank Thee for sleep (1809); Gilbert, Ann
*My Father is the mighty Lord (1854); Findlater, Sarah
 My Father, when around me spread (1828); Hornblower, Jane
 My goal is God Himself (1896); Brook, Frances
*My God, again the morning breaketh (1863); Manington, Alice
 My God, all nature owns Thy sway (1786); Williams, Helen
 My God, and can I linger still (1835); Elliott, Julia
 My God and Father! while I stray (1834); Elliott, Charlotte
*My God, behold me lying (1863); Winkworth, Catherine
 My God has given me work to do (1849); Bourdillon, Mary
*My God! I know full well that I must die (1858); Warner, Anna
*My God! I know that I must die (1854); Findlater, Sarah
*My God, in Thee all fulness lies (1858); Winkworth, Catherine

My God, is any hour so sweet? (1836); Elliott, Charlotte
*My God, lo, here before Thy face (1855); Winkworth, Catherine
My God, O let me call Thee mine (1846); Brontë, Anne
My God, shall I for ever mourn (1769); Scott, Elizabeth
*My God, Thou hast the invite given (1863); Manington, Alice
My God, 'tis to Thy mercy-seat (1760); Steele, Anne
*My God, to Thee I now command (1855); Winkworth, Catherine
*My God! when will Thy heavenly peace (1843); Fortesque, Eleanor
*My God with me in every place (1854); Findlater, Sarah
*My God, within Thy hand (1858); Warner, Anne
*My heart awakes with holy glee (1863); Manington, Alice
*My heart is bright with joy (1873); Durand, Emily
*My heart is filled with longing (1863); Winkworth, Catherine
*My heart wakes with a joyful lay (1862); Findlater, Sarah
My home is God Himself (1899); Brook, Frances
*My inmost heart now raises (1863); Winkworth, Catherine
*My Jesus, as Thou wilt (1854); Borthwick, Jane
*My Jesus, if the seraphim (1858); Winkworth, Catherine
*My Jesus the sinner receives (1869); Warner, Anna
*My joy is wholly banished (1869); Winkworth, Catherine
*My joy was ne'er unmixed with care (1869); Winkworth, Catherine
My Maker and my King; to Thee my whole I owe (1760); Steele,
    Anne
My only Saviour, when I fell (1835); Elliott, Charlotte
*My restless heart, with anguish moaning (1841); Cox, Frances
My Saviour, be Thou near me (1839, 1841); Duncan, Mary
My Saviour, I would own Thee (1873); Taylor, Rebekah
*My Saviour lives, and He the might (1863); Manington, Alice
*My Saviour lives! I will rejoice (1843); Fortesque, Eleanor
*My Saviour, make me cleave to Thee (1841); Cox, Frances
My Saviour, 'mid life's varied scene (1873); Godwin, Elizabeth
My Saviour, on the words of truth (1850); Waring, Anna
*My Shepherd is the Saviour dear (1857); Dunn, Catherine
*My soul adores the might of loving (1867); Ashley, Mrs. E.
My soul awake! Thy rest forsake (1880); Livock, Jane
My soul complete in Jesus stands (1855, 1865); Hinsdale, Grace
*My soul hath found the steadfast ground (1858); Bevan, Emma
*My soul is thirsty, Lord, for Thee (1843); Fortesque, Eleanor
*My soul! let this your thoughts employ (1841); Cox, Frances
*My soul, now praise thy maker (1863); Winkworth, Catherine
*My soul, thy great Redeemer see (1864); Borthwick, Jane
My span of life will soon be done (1792); Cowper, Frances
*My whole desire doth briefly turn away (1869); Warner, Anna

Nearer, my God, to Thee (1841); Adams, Sarah
Never be faint or weary (1873); Van Alstyne, Frances
*Never couldst Thou bear to grieve us (1854); Borthwick, Jane
Never forget what God has done (1959); Bechtel, Helen

Never further than Thy Cross (1860); Charles, Elizabeth
*New mercies, new blessings, new light on Thy way (1874);
    Havergal, Frances
*Night from the earth is wending (1863); Manington, Alice
 No cloud obscures the summer's sky (1827); Hemans, Felicia
 No evil shall befall (1861); Maurice, Jane
 No Gospel like this Feast (1859); Charles, Elizabeth
 None but Christ; His merit hides me (1876); Cousin, Anne
 None other lamb, none other name (1892); Rossetti, Christina
 Not for the summer hour alone (1841); Sigourney, Lydia
*Not in anger, mighty God (1863); Winkworth, Catherine
*Not in anger, smite us, Lord (1855); Winkworth, Catherine
*Not more than I have strength to bear (1858); Warner, Anna
 Not now, my child; a little more rough tossing (1873); Penne-
    father, Catherine
 Not only as a sacrifice (1841); Yonge, Frances
 Not only for the goodly fruit-trees fall (1881); Armitage, Ella
*Not so darkly, not so deep (1858); Warner, Anna
 Not Thy garment's hem alone (1836); Conder, Joan
 Not willingly dost Thou afflict (1841); Elliott, Charlotte
 Not your own, but His ye are (1867, 1869); Havergal, Frances
 Nothing but leaves, the Spirit grieves (1858); Akerman, Lucy
*Nothing fair on earth I see (1855); Winkworth, Catherine
*Now all the woods are sleeping (1856); Winkworth, Catherine
*Now at last I end the strife (1858); Winkworth, Catherine
 Now autumn strews on every plain (1808); Hemans, Felicia
*Now awake my soul, my senses (1864); Borthwick, Jane
 Now condescend, Almighty King (1809); Taylor, Jane
*Now darkness over all is spread (1858); Winkworth, Catherine
*Now every greenwood sleepeth (1863); Manington, Alice
*Now fain my joyous heart would sing (1858); Winkworth, Catherine
*Now God be praised, and God alone (1869); Winkworth, Catherine
*Now God be with us, for the night is closing (1863); Winkworth,
    Catherine
*Now heavy heart, away with sorrow (1863); Manington, Alice
*Now I close my tired eyes (1859); Bevan, Emma
*Now I find a lasting joy (1864); Borthwick, Jane
*Now I live; but if to night (1858); Warner, Anna
*Now, in peace of God (1875); Borthwick, Jane
*Now lay we calmly in the grave (1858); Winkworth, Catherine
 Now let our heavenly plants and flowers (1838); Elliott,
    Charlotte
*Now let us loudly (1863); Winkworth, Catherine
*Now let us pray the Holy Ghost (1869); Winkworth, Catherine
 Now let us sing the angels' song (1879); Havergal, Frances
 Now lettest Thou Thy servant Lord (1853); Leeson, Jane
*Now may our God, His mercy (1845); Fry, Henrietta
 Now one day's journey less divides (1836); Elliott, Charlotte

*Now rest the woods again (1855); Winkworth, Catherine
*Now rests her soul in Jesus' arms (1855); Winkworth, Catherine
*Now soon I shall have conquer'd (1863); Manington, Alice
*Now take my heart and all that is in me (1858); Winkworth,
    Catherine
*Now thank we all our God (1858); Winkworth, Catherine
 Now that my journey's just begun (1810); Taylor, Jane
*Now that the day from earth hath crept (1863); Manington,
    Alice
*Now that the sun doth shine no more (1863); Winkworth, Catherine
 Now the blessed dayspring (1890); Thomson, Mary
 Now the daylight goes away (1869, 1870); Havergal, Frances
 Now the days are dark and dreary (1885); Hawkins, Hester
 Now the Lord our souls has fed (1899); Marston, Annie
*Now the Saviour of the heathen (1845); Fry, Henrietta
 Now the six days' work is done (1879); Hernaman, Claudia
 Now the solemn shadows darken (1881); Doudney, Sarah
 Now the sowing and the weeping (1870); Havergal, Frances
 Now the year is crowned with blessing (1904); Felkin, Ellen
*Now warneth us the wise man's fare (1869); Winkworth, Catherine
*Now we must leave our Fatherland (1858); Winkworth, Catherine
*Now weary heart! thy care dismiss (1843); Fortesque, Eleanor
*Now weeping at the grave we stand (1858); Winkworth, Catherine
*Now will I nevermore despair of Heaven (1869); Winkworth,
    Catherine

 O all ye lands, rejoice in God (1829); Auber, Harriet
*O anxious care that weighs me down (1865); Burlingham, Hannah
*O beautiful abode of earth (1858); Warner, Anna
 O beautiful for spacious skies (1893, 1899); Bates, Katharine
*O blessed are ye messengers, sent forth (1873); Durand, Emily
*O blessed Jesus! (1858); Winkworth, Catherine
*O Blessed Saviour! here we meet (1843); Fortesque, Eleanor
 O breath of life, come sweeping through us (1914); Head, Bessie
 O Christ, forget not them who stand (n.d.); Sangster, Margaret
 O! Christ He is the fountain (1857); Cousin, Anne
*O Christ! how good and fair (1858); Charles, Elizabeth
*O Christ, my life, my Saviour (1875); Borthwick, Jane
*O Christ, the leader of that war-torn host (1857); Winkworth,
    Catherine
*O Christ, Thou bright and morning star (1858); Winkworth,
    Catherine
 O Christ, what burdens bowed Thy head (1876); Cousin, Anne
*O come, my soul, with singing (1866); Burlingham, Hannah
 O come to the Saviour, believe in His name (1874, 1875); Van
    Alstyne, Frances
 O come with God and worship God (1959); Bechtel, Helen
*O cross, we hail thy bitter reign (1855); Winkworth, Catherine

O day of joy and wonder (1957, 1965); Buchanan, Violet
*O day! that hast unto our souls set forth (1859); Fry, Henrietta
 O day to sweet religious thought (1866); Cary, Alice
 O do not let the word depart (1842); Reed, Eliza
*O enter, Lord, Thy temple (1863); Winkworth, Catherine
*O everlasting source of life and light (1862); Borthwick, Jane
 O faint and feeble-hearted (1836); Elliott, Charlotte
*O faithful Saviour, Jesus Christ (1863); Manington, Alice
*O faithful Shepherd! now behold (1843); Fortesque, Eleanor
 O Father, ere the night draw near (1903); Leefe, Isabella
 O Father, in Thy Father's heart (1887); Armitage, Ella
*O Father, Son, and Holy Ghost, Thou God, dost fix the miner's
     post (1869); Winkworth, Catherine
 O Father, though the anxious fear (1818); Taylor, Emily
 O Father, to the fields that are ripe (1832); Gould, Hannah
 O Father, we are very weak (1879); Brawn, Mary
 O Father, we would thank Thee (1904); Greenaway, Ada
 O Father, whom in truth to know (1870); Toke, Emma
*O Father-eye, that hath so truly watched (1858); Winkworth,
     Catherine
*O Father-heart, Who hast created all (1858); Winkworth,
     Catherine
*O fear not, Christians, that rough path to tread (1864); Cox,
     Frances
*O fire of love, what earthly words (1858); Bevan, Emma
*O foolish heart, be still (1858); Warner, Anna
 O for the peace which floweth as a river (1860); Crewdson, Jane
 O for the robes of whiteness (1860); Bancroft, Charitie
 O Fount of life and beauty (1878); Wiglesworth, Esther
*O friend of souls, how well is me (1855); Winkworth, Catherine
 O from the world's vile slavery (1815); Cotterill, Jane
 O garden of Olivet, dear honour'd spot (1791); DeFleury, Maria
 O gentle Jesus, had I been (1862); Clare, Mary
 O gentle presence, peace (n.d.); Eddy, Mary
*O gentle Shepherd by Thy staff directed (1865); Burlingham,
     Hannah
*O gentle Shepherd, guided by Thy hand (1853); Dunn, Catherine
 O, glorious God and King (1872, 1874); Havergal, Frances
*O glorious Head, Thou livest now (1855); Winkworth, Catherine
*O God, I long Thy light to see (1855); Winkworth, Catherine
 O God, I thank Thee for each night (1875); Mason, Caroline
 O God, may I look up to Thee (1841); Elliott, Charlotte
*O God, my heart is fixed on Thee (1858); Charles, Elizabeth
*O God, O Spirit, light of all that live (1855); Winkworth,
     Catherine
*O God, O Spirit, Light of life (1858); Bevan, Emma
 O God of ages in whose light (1888); Jarvis, Mary
 O God of comfort, Thou alone (1870); Toke, Emma

O God of Israel, deign to smile (n.d.); Tonna, Charlotte
O God of light, Thy word (1952); Taylor, Sarah
O God of mercy, chill and dark (1870); Toke, Emma
O God of mercy! hearken now (1891); Clark, Emily
O God, our Father, Ruler of the nations (1975); Jordan, Diane
O God, our Saviour, from Thy birth (1855); Walker, Mary
O God our strength, to Thee the song (1829); Auber, Harriet
O God, the strength and stay of all (1870); Toke, Emma
*O God, Thou faithful God (1858); Winkworth, Catherine
O God, Thy Church eternal (1969); Hardcastle, Carrie
O God, Thy world is sweet with prayer (1892); Larcom, Lucy
O God, to Thee we raise our eyes (1804); Richardson, Charlotte
O God, to Thee, Who first hast given (1820); Hornblower, Jane
*O God! uphold us by Thy word, and scatter (1845); Fry, Henrietta
O God, upon this solemn day (1870); Toke, Emma
*O God, whose attributes shine forth in turn (1864); Cox, Frances
*O good beyond compare (1869); Winkworth, Catherine
*O great and gracious God (1864); Borthwick, Jane
O hallowed memories of the past (1841); Adams, Sarah
O happy land, O happy land (1840); Parson, Elizabeth
O happy souls that love the Lord (1780); Harrison, Susanna
O happy they who safely housed (1842); Gilbert, Ann
*O Head, blood-stained and wounded (1857); Dunn, Catherine
O hear my cry, be gracious now to me (1877); Van Alstyne,
    Frances
O heart of Jesus, heart of God (1872); Fullerton, Georgiana
O help me, Lord, this day to be (1881); Butler, Mary
O here, if ever, God of love (1818); Taylor, Emily
O Holy Ghost, the comforter (1849); Saxby, Jane
*O Holy Ghost! Thou fire divine (1855); Winkworth, Catherine
*O Holy Ghost! Thy heavenly dew (1841); Cox, Frances
*O Holy Spirit, enter in (1863); Winkworth, Catherine
O Holy Spirit, now descend on me (1861); Forsyth, Christina
*O how blest are ye beyond our telling (1863); Winkworth,
    Catherine
*O how blest who, all resigning (1865); Smith, Mrs. L.C.
*O how many an hour of gladness (1873); Durand, Emily
*O how sweet it is to pray (1859); Bevan, Emma
O human heart! thou hast a song (1841); Adams, Sarah
O I would sing a song of praise (1841); Adams, Sarah
*O Jesu Christ, most good, most fair (1869); Winkworth, Catherine
O Jesu, it were surely sweet (1853); Caddell, Cecelia
O Jesu, Thou art present (1880); Leefe, Isabella
*O Jesus, at Thy shining (1865); Burlingham, Hannah
O Jesus bruised and wounded more (1859); Alexander, Cecil
*O Jesus Christ, grow Thou in me (1860); Smith, Elizabeth
*O Jesus Christ, my sunshine (1864); Manington, Alice
O Jesus Christ, the holy One (1867); Saxby, Jane
*O Jesus Christ, Thy cradle is (1864); Manington, Alice

O Jesus, dearest Lord, I cry to Thee (1876); Shapcote, Emily
*O Jesus, Friend unfailing (1865); Burlingham, Hannah
O Jesus, Jesus, my good Lord (1742); Taylor, Clare
O Jesus, make Thyself to me (1862, 1872); Elliott, Charlotte
O Jesus, who once heard the plea (1961); Price, Marion
O joyful tidings let us sing (1855); Walker, Mary
*O King of Glory, David's son (1858); Winkworth, Catherine
O King of Saints, we give (1890); Thomson, Mary
*O Lamb of God, most stainless (1863); Winkworth, Catherine
O Lamb of God that tak'st away (1865); Faussett, Alessie
O Lamb of God, who dost abide (1884); Hernaman, Claudia
*O! let him whose sorrow (1841); Cox, Frances
O let me praise my God and King (1871); Villiers, Margaret
O let your mingling voices rise (1845); Jarvis, Mary
*O light, who out of light wast born (1869); Winkworth, Catherine
O little birds, that all day long (1880); Matheson, Annie
O little child, lie still and sleep (1867); Warner, Anna
*O living bread from Heaven (1858); Winkworth, Catherine
O living Christ, chief cornerstone (1935); Cunninggim, Maude
*O Lord, be this our vessel now (1858); Winkworth, Catherine
O Lord, I come to Thee (1890); Marston, Annie
*O Lord! I long Thy face to see (1841); Cox, Frances
O Lord, in all our travels here (1851, 1852); Toke, Emma
*O Lord, my God, I cry to Thee (1858); Winkworth, Catherine
O Lord of all, we bring to Thee (1879, 1881); Armitage, Ella
O Lord of hosts, the fight is long (1894); Armitage, Ella
O Lord of life, and love, and power (1875, 1881); Armitage, Ella
O Lord our banner, God of might (1884); Wordsworth, Elizabeth
*O Lord our God! to Thee we raise, One universal (1845); Fry,
    Henrietta
O Lord, our God, whom all through life we praise (n.d.); Winters
    Frances
O Lord, the contrite sinner's friend (1742); Taylor, Clare
O Lord, Thou knowest all the snares (1851, 1852); Toke, Emma
*O Lord, Thy goodness we adore (1843); Fortesque, Eleanor
O Lord, Thy work revive (1819, 1831); Brown, Phoebe
O Lord, we know it matters not (1842); Peters, Mary
O Lord, whilst we confess the worth (1847); Peters, Mary
O Lord, wilt Thou teach me to pray? (1813); Taylor, Jane
O Lord, with Thee 'tis but a little matter (1896); Brook, France
*O Love, thou makest all things even (1841); Adams, Sarah
*O Love, Who formedst me to wear (1858); Winkworth, Catherine
O lovely voices of the sky (1827); Hemans, Felicia
O Master, at Thy feet (1866, 1867); Havergal, Frances
O Master! when Thou callest (1888); Stock, Sarah
O may the truths this day has taught (n.d.); Daye, Elizabeth
*O mighty Spirit! source whence all things sprung (1858); Wink-
    worth, Catherine

*O Morning Star! how fair and bright (1863); Winkworth, Catherine
 O my adored Redeemer! deign to be (1755); Masters, Mary
 O my Father, I would know Thee (1894); Munger, Harriet
 O my God, I fear Thee (1881); Dobree, Henrietta
*O my heart, be calm and patient (1864); Borthwick, Jane
*O my heart, be calm, confiding (1866); Burlingham, Hannah
 O my Saviour, hear me (1875); Van Alstyne, Frances
*O my soul be glad and cheerful (1863); Winkworth, Catherine
 O not for these alone I pray (1826); Taylor, Emily
 O not when o'er the trembling soul (1835); Elliott, Julia
 O perfect God, Thy love (1902, 1904); Greenaway, Ada
 O perfect love, all human thought transcending (1883, 1889);
      Gurney, Dorothy
 O praise our great and gracious Lord (1829); Auber, Harriet
*O precious Jesus, what hast Thou been doing (1865); Burlingham,
      Hannah
*O rejoice, ye Christians, loudly (1863); Winkworth, Catherine
*O risen Lord! O conquering King! (1858); Winkworth, Catherine
*O rose! of the flowers, I ween, thou art fairest (1869);
      Winkworth, Catherine
 O Saviour Christ, Who art Thyself (1882); Roberts, Martha
 O Saviour, I have nought to plead (1864); Crewdson, Jane
 O Saviour, precious Saviour (1870); Havergal, Frances
 O Saviour, where shall guilty man (1858); May, Catherine
 O sing to me of heaven (1840); Dana, Mary
 O Sion, haste, Thy mission high fulfilling (1892); Thomson, Mary
 O Son of Man! Great Sower (1893); Pearce, Lydia
 O Son of man, who walked each day (1928); Turner, Nancy
*O soul why dost thou weary (1869); Warner, Anna
 O source of good! around me spread (1826); Taylor, Emily
 O spirit freed from earth (1834); Howitt, Mary
 O Spirit, whose name is the Saviour (1881); Larcom, Lucy
 O spotless Lamb of God, in Thee (1855); Walker, Mary
 O spouse of Christ, on whom (1881); Drane, Augusta
 O sun of truth and glory (1882); Whiting, Mary
*O sweet home echo on the pilgrim's way (1858); Borthwick, Jane
*O tell me not of gold and treasure (1865); Burlingham, Hannah
*O that day, that day of ire (1851); Preston, Mrs. M.J.
 O that I could for ever dwell (1842); Reed, Eliza
 O the clanging bells of time (n.d.); Gates, Ellen
 O this is blessing, this is rest (1854); Waring, Anna
*O Thou blessed light of light (1857); Dunn, Catherine
 O Thou blest Lamb of God (1858); Morris, Eliza
 O Thou chosen Church of Jesus (1871, 1874); Havergal, Frances
*O Thou essential Word (1855); Winkworth, Catherine
 O Thou Lord of heaven above (n.d.); Waring, Anna
*O Thou most highest! Guardian of mankind (1858); Winkworth,
      Catherine

*O Thou of God the Father (1863); Winkworth, Catherine
 O Thou, the contrite sinner's friend (1835); Elliott, Charlotte
 O Thou the great unknown unseen (1885); Hawkins, Hester
 O Thou, to whose all seeing eye (1852); Toke, Emma
*O Thou, true God alone (1869); Winkworth, Catherine
 O Thou, Who are for our fallen race (1841); Hastings, Flora
 O Thou Who art in every place (1850); Brawn, Mary
 O Thou who didst prepare (1829); Tonna, Charlotte
 O Thou, who didst this rite reveal (1835); Elliott, Julia
 O Thou, Who didst through heavens (1870); Toke, Emma
 O Thou, Who didst with love untold (1851, 1852); Toke, Emma
 O Thou! Who has at Thy command (1815); Cotterill, Jane
 O Thou who hast spread out the skies (1832); Gould, Hanna
 O Thou Whom heaven's bright host revere (1829); Auber, Harriet
 O Thou whose bounty fills my cup (1860); Crewdson, Jane
 O to be over yonder (1862, 1865); Armstrong, Florence
*O watchman, will the night of sin (1855); Winkworth, Catherine
*O weep not, mourn not this bier (1855); Winkworth, Catherine
*O well for him who all things braves (1855); Winkworth, Catherin
 O what a happy lot is mine (1861); Forsyth, Christina
 O what are you going to do, brother? (1868); Van Alstyne, France
 O what everlasting blessings God out poureth on His own (1871);
        Havergal, Frances
*O what joy for them is stored (1858); Bevan, Emma
 O! when shall I sweep through the gates (1878); Palmer, Phoebe
 O when shall their souls find a rest? (1893); Stock, Sarah
*O will of God, all sweet and perfect (1873); Durand, Emily
 O word of love! O word of life (1882); Whitney, Mary
 O word of pity, for our pardon pleading (1904); Greenaway, Ada
*O world! behold upon the tree (1858); Winkworth, Catherine
*O world, I must forsake thee (1869); Winkworth, Catherine
*O world, I now must leave thee (1863); Winkworth, Catherine
 O world of pride, throw open wide (1887); Thwaites, Clara
*O would, my God, that I could praise Thee (1863); Winkworth,
        Catherine
*O wouldst Thou, in Thy glory, come (1858); Winkworth, Catherine
*O ye halls of heaven (1869); Winkworth, Catherine
*O ye who bear your Saviour's name (1843); Fortesque, Eleanor
*O ye who from earliest youth (1869); Winkworth, Catherine
*O ye your Saviour's name who bear (1841); Cox, Frances
 O'er life's tempestuous sea (1850); Brawn, Mary
 O'er waiting harp-strings (n.d.); Eddy, Mary
*Of all the golden hours whose light (1841); Lowe, Helen
*Of all the joys that are on earth (1869); Winkworth, Catherine
 Of all the thoughts of God, that are; Browning, Elizabeth
 Often the clouds of deepest woe (1821); Wilson, Caroline
*Oh blest the house, whate'er befall (1863); Winkworth, Catherine
*Oh! could I but be still (1859); Bevan, Emma
*Oh! could my soul possess His love (1845); Fry, Henrietta

*Oh! how blessed are ye, saints forgiven (1854); Borthwick, Jane
*Oh how could I forget Him? (1858); Winkworth, Catherine
*Oh, let Thy praise, Redeemer, God! (1845); Fry, Henrietta
*Oh Lord our God, from Heaven look down (1845); Fry, Henrietta
*Oh Lord! Thy presence through the day's distractions (1859);
    Fry, Henrietta
*Oh! love that did the heavens rend asunder (1864); Manington,
    Alice
*Oh! sweetest words that Jesus could have sought (1855); Find-
    later, Sarah
*Oh! what is human life below (1864); Cox, Frances
*Oh would I had a thousand tongues (1855); Winkworth, Catherine
*On the dewy breath of even (1835); Elliott, Julia
*On this day, earth shall ring (n.d.); Joseph, Jane
 On Thy Church, O power divine (1829); Auber, Harriet
*On wings of faith, ye thoughts, fly hence (1855); Winkworth,
    Catherine
*Once a merchant travelled far and wide (1855); Borthwick, Jane
*Once again to its close (n.d.); Drury, Miriam
*Once He came in blessing (1863); Winkworth, Catherine
 Once I thought to sit so high (1863); Rossetti, Christina
 Once in royal David's city (1848); Alexander, Cecil
*Once in the bands of death the Saviour lay (1845); Fry, Henrietta
*Once more from rest I rise again (1855); Winkworth, Catherine
*Once more the day-light shines abroad (1858); Winkworth,
    Catherine
 Once pledged by the Cross (1901); Bode, Alice
 Once Thy servants toiled in rowing (1892); Stock, Sarah
 Once to our world there came (1857); Strafford, Elizabeth
 Once upon the heaving ocean (n.d.); Dana, Mary
 One by one the sands are going (1858); Procter, Adelaide
 One by one we cross the river (1866); Baxter, Lydia
 One fervent wish, my God (1867); Shekleton, Mary
 One more boundary passed o'er (1873); Taylor, Rebekah
 One more day's work for Jesus (1869); Warner, Anna
*One more flying moment (1873); Durand, Emily
*One, only one, shall be the fold (1857); Dunn, Catherine
 One sweetly solemn thought (1852); Cary, Phoebe
 One there is above all others (1817); Nunn, Marianne
*One thing is needful! let me deem (1855); Winkworth, Catherine
*One thing's needful, then, Lord Jesus (1841); Cox, Frances
*One touch from Thee, the Healer of diseases (1864); Crewdson,
    Jane
 Only a little while (n.d.); Crozier, Maria
 Only a step to Jesus (1873); Van Alstyne, Frances
 Only Jesus feels and knows (1875); Van Alstyne, Frances
 Only waiting till the shadows (1854); Mace, Frances
 Onward, onward, men of heaven (1833); Sigourney, Lydia
*Open my eyes, that I may see (1895); Scott, Clara

*Open now Thy gates of beauty (1863); Winkworth, Catherine
 Open stood the gates of heaven (n.d.); Stock, Sarah
 Open your hearts as a flower to the light (1892); Larcom, Lucy
 Oppressed with sin and woe (1846); Brontë, Anne
*Our beloved have departed (1855); Findlater, Sarah
 Our blest Redeemer, ere He breathed (1829); Auber, Harriet
 Our Church proclaims God's love and care (1939); McCaw, Mabel
 Our country is Immanuel's ground (1792); Barbauld, Anna
 Our country's voice is pleading (1849); Anderson, Maria
 Our days are few and full of strife (1866); Cary, Alice
*Our dear Lord of grace hath given (1869); Winkworth, Catherine
 Our dear Lord's garden (1881); Armitage, Ella
 Our Father in heaven, we hallow Thy name (1831); Hale, Sarah
*Our Father in the heavenly realm (1845); Fry, Henrietta
 Our Father, our Father, Who dwellest in light (1872, 1874);
     Havergal, Frances
*Our Father, Thou in heaven above (1863); Winkworth, Catherine
 Our God is light, we do not go (1847); Peters, Mary
*Our God, our Father (1858); Winkworth, Catherine
 Our heavenly Father is not known (1742); Taylor, Clare
 Our pilgrim brethren, dwelling far (1844); Livermore, Sarah
 Our Saviour and our King (1871); Havergal, Frances
 Our Saviour's voice is soft and sweet (1858); Parson, Elizabeth
 Our solemn Lent has come again (1881); Dobree, Henrietta
 Our thoughts go round the world (1963); Moore, Jessie
*Out from the east the golden morn is rising (1863); Manington,
     Alice
*Out of the depths I cry to Thee, Lord God! (1855); Winkworth,
     Catherine
 Out of the depths to Thee I cry (1877); Marcy, Elizabeth

 Pain and toil are over now (1846); Alexander, Cecil
 Paraphrases of the Psalms (1667); Beale, Mary
 Part in peace! Christ's life was peace (1841); Adams, Sarah
 Part in peace! is day before us? (1841); Adams, Sarah
 Pass away, earthly joy (1844); Bonar, Jane
 Pass me not, O gentle Saviour (1870); Van Alstyne, Frances
 Pastor, thou art from us taken (1836); Sigourney, Lydia
*Patience and humility (1869); Winkworth, Catherine
*Peace, be still, through the night (1875); Borthwick, Jane
 Poor and needy though I be (1836); Thrupp, Dorothy
 Poor wanderer, return to the home of thy bliss (1839, 1842);
     Cockburn-Campbell, Margaret
 Pour Thy blessings, Lord (1866); Kimball, Harriet
*Praise and thanks to Thee be sung (1855); Winkworth, Catherine
 Praise for the Garden of God upon earth (1881); Armitage, Ella
 Praise for the glorious light (1844); Hale, Mary
*Praise God, now Christians all alike (1864); Manington, Alice
 Praise God, ye gladdening smiles of morn (n.d.); Shipton, Anna
 Praise Him, praise Him (1869); Van Alstyne, Frances

Praise the Lord, our mighty King (1829); Auber, Harriet
Praise the Lord, sing Hallelujah (1864); Heath, Eliza
Praise to God, immortal praise (1772); Barbauld, Anna
*Praise to Jehovah! the Almighty King of Creation (1855); Borth-
    wick, Jane
*Praise to the Lord! the Almighty, the King of Creation (1863);
    Winkworth, Catherine
*Praise to Thee, O Lord, most holy (1872); Chester, Henrietta
Praise ye Jehovah, praise the Lord most holy (1838, 1842);
    Cockburn-Campbell, Margaret
Praise ye the Lord, again, again (1847); Peters, Mary
Praise ye the Lord on every height (1827); Hemans, Felicia
Prayer is the dew of faith (n.d.); Sigourney, Lydia
Precious, precious blood of Jesus (1874); Havergal, Frances
*Prepare me now my narrow bed (1843); Fortesque, Eleanor
Present the two or three (1871); Freer, Frances
Press on! press on! a glorious throng (1869); Van Alstyne,
    Frances
Prince of Peace, control my will (1858); Dana, Mary
*Prince of Peace! Thy name confessing (1866); Burlingham, Hannah
Proclaim the lofty praise (1829); Judson, Sarah
*Pure Essence! spotless Fount of light (1855); Winkworth,
    Catherine
Pure spirit, O where art Thou now? (1808, 1825); Barbauld, Anna
Put far from us, O Lord we pray (1841); Yonge, Frances

Queen of the Holy Rosary (1882); Shapcote, Emily
Quiet from God! it cometh not to still (1834); Williams, Sarah J.

Rabboni, Master, we have heard (1895); Elliott, Emily
*Raise high the notes of exultation (1841); Cox, Frances
*Redeemer of the nations, come (1858); Charles, Elizabeth
*Redeemer of the nations, come (1855); Winkworth, Catherine
*Rejoice, all ye believers (1854); Findlater, Sarah
*Rejoice, dear Christendom to-day (1869); Winkworth, Catherine
Rejoice, my fellow pilgrim (1859); Borthwick, Jane
*Rejoice, rejoice, ye Christians (1863); Winkworth, Catherine
*Rejoice, that rest is not far distant (1863); Manington, Alice
*Remember me, my God! remember me! (1854); Borthwick, Jane
*Rescue the perishing, care for the dying (1870); Van Alstyne,
    Frances
Rest, weary heart: the penalty is borne (1859); Borthwick, Jane
Rest, weary soul (1864); Borthwick, Jane
Restore, O Father, to our times restore (1837); Popple, Maria
*Return! return! poor long-lost wanderer, home (1855); Borth-
    wick, Jane
*Return, return, Thou lost one (1873); Durand, Emily
Reverently we worship Thee (1873); Hernaman, Claudia
Revive Thy work, O Lord (1875); Van Alstyne, Frances
Ring, happy bells of Easter time (1892); Larcom, Lucy

*Rise again! yes rise again wilt Thou (1869); Winkworth, Catherine
*Rise again! yes, Thou shalt rise again, my dust (1859); Fry,
    Henrietta
*Rise, follow Me! our Master saith (1863); Winkworth, Catherine
 Rise, for the day is passing (1858); Procter, Adelaide
*Rise, my soul, Thy vigil keep (1857); Dunn, Catherine
*Rise, my soul, to watch and pray (1863); Winkworth, Catherine
 Rise, O British nation, hasten now to pay (1886); Roberts,
    Martha
*Rise, ye children of salvation (1858); Bevan, Emma
 Rocked in the cradle of the deep (1830); Willard, Emma
*Round their planets roll the moons (1869); Winkworth, Catherine
 Round Thy footstool, Saviour, see (1896); Stock, Sarah

*Sad with longing, sick with fears (1858); Winkworth, Catherine
 Safe in the arms of Jesus (1868, 1869); Van Alstyne, Frances
 Safely, safely gathered in (1881); Dobree, Henrietta
 Saints of God! the dawn is brightening (1849); Maxwell, Mary
 Salt of the earth, ye virtuous few (1825); Barbauld, Anna
*Salvation hath come down to us (1869); Winkworth, Catherine
 Salvation to our God (1847); Peters, Mary
 Saviour, be Thy sweet compassion (1865); Cross, Ada
 Saviour, bless a little child (1869); Van Alstyne, Frances
 Saviour, for the little one (1892); Thomason, Mary
 Saviour, hear us, as we plead (1897); Greenaway, Ada
 Saviour, more than life for me (1875); Van Alstyne, Frances
 Saviour, now receive him (1834); Hemans, Felicia
 Saviour, now the day is ending (1871); Doudney, Sarah
*Saviour of sinners, now revive us (1864); Borthwick, Jane
 Saviour, round Thy footstool bending (1840); Parson, Elizabeth
 Saviour, shed Thy sweetest blessing (1865); Cousin, Anne
 Saviour, teach me day by day (1842); Leeson, Jane
 Saviour, Thy law we love (1832); Sigourney, Lydia
 Saviour, to Whom the sound of sorrows sighing (1899); Fox,
    Eleanor
 Saviour, where dwellest Thou? (1858); Clapham, Emma
 Saw ye my Saviour? (n.d.); Eddy, Mary
 Saw you never in the twilight (1853); Alexander, Cecil
 Say, is your lamp burning, my brother (n.d.); Gates, Ellen
 Say, sinner, hath a voice within? (1824); Hyde, Abby
 Say, where is thy refuge, my brother? (1874); Van Alstyne,
    Frances
*See, bowed beneath a fearful weight (1857); Dunn, Catherine
 See, gracious God, before Thy throne (1756, 1760); Steele,
    Anne
 "See how he loved," exclaimed the Jews (1812); Bache, Sarah
 See how the rising sun (1806); Scott, Elizabeth
 See in the vineyard of the Lord (1795); Wilkinson, Rebecca

See, my child, the mighty ocean (1836); Thrupp, Dorothy
See the kind Shepherd, Jesus, stands (1795); Wilkinson, Rebecca
*See! Triumphant over death (1845); Fry, Henrietta
*See what a man is this, O glances (1869); Warner, Anna
*See! what wondrous love, how matchless (1863); Manington, Alice
See where the gentle Jesus reigns (1847); Shepherd, Anne
*Seeing I am Jesus' lamb (1858); Winkworth, Catherine
*Seems it in my anguish lone (1858); Winkworth, Catherine
Send Thou, O Lord, to every place (1890); Gates, Mary
Serve the Lord with joy and gladness (1959); Huey, Mary
*Seven times our blessed Saviour spoke (1841); Cox, Frances
*Shall I not sing praise to Thee (1855); Winkworth, Catherine
*Shall I not trust my God (1858); Warner, Anna
*Shall I o'er the future fret (1869); Winkworth, Catherine
Shed Thou, O Lord, Thy light (1945); Harkness, Georgia
Shepherd, show me how to go (n.d.); Eddy, Mary
Shepherd, who Thy life didst give (1878); Hernaman, Claudia
*Should I not be meek and still (1858); Bevan, Emma
Show me the way, O Lord (1849); Saxby, Jane
Shrouded once in blackest night (1827); Herschell, Esther
Shut out from heaven's glory (n.d.); Stock, Sarah
Silence, O earth, and listen to the song (n.d.); Chant, Laura
*Since Christ is gone to heaven, His home (1858); Winkworth,
    Catherine
*Since I one day from yonder sleeping (1869); Warner, Anna
*Since Thou, the living God, art Three (1845); Fry, Henrietta
Sing for the Lord! for his mercies are sure (1841); Adams,
    Sarah
Sing, for the world rejoiceth (1887); Hearn, Marianne
Sing, O heavens, the Lord hath done it (1879); Havergal, Frances
*Sing praise to God who reigns above (1864); Cox, Frances
Singing for Jesus, our Saviour and King (1872, 1874); Havergal,
    Frances
*Sink not yet, my soul, to slumber (1858); Winkworth, Catherine
Sinner, what hast thou to show? (1829); Tonna, Charlotte
*Sinners, Jesus will receive (1858); Bevan, Emma
Sit down beneath His shadow (1870); Havergal, Frances
*Sleep not, O soul by God awakened (1873); Durand, Emily
Sleep, sleep to-day, tormenting cares (1807); Barbauld, Anna
*Small amongst cities, Bethlehem (1858); Charles, Elizabeth
So be it, Lord, the prayers are prayed (1848); Alexander, Cecil
Softly on the breath of evening (1864); Van Alstyne, Frances
Soldier, go, but not to claim (n.d.); Tonna, Charlotte
Someone shall go at the Master's word (1893); Stock, Sarah
*Something every heart is loving (1858); Bevan, Emma
Songs of glory fill the sky (1864); Leeson, Jane
*Soon night the world in gloom will sleep (1863); Manington, Alice
*Soon shall that voice resound (1845); Fry, Henrietta

Soon, too soon, the sweet repose (1835); Elliott, Julia
*Soul, arise, dispel thy sadness (1864); Borthwick, Jane
*Soul! couldst Thou, while on earth remaining (1841); Cox, Frances
Souls in heathen darkness lying (1851); Alexander, Cecil
Sound the alarm! let the watchman cry (1880); Van Alstyne,
    Frances
Source of my life's refreshing springs (1850); Waring, Anna
Sovereign Lord and gracious Master (1871, 1872); Havergal,
    Frances
Sowers went throughout the land (1872); Elliott, Emily
Spared to another spring (1827); Gilbert, Ann
Speak the truth, for that is right (1871); Villiers, Margaret
Spirit of God, that moved of old (1852); Alexander, Cecil
Spirit of Peace, who as a dove (1829); Auber, Harriet
Spirit of truth, be Thou my guide (1846); Brontë, Anne
*Spread, oh spread, Thou mighty word (1858); Winkworth, Catherine
Stand we prepared to see and hear (1864); Leeson, Jane
Standing at the portal of the opening year (1873, 1874);
    Havergal, Frances
Star of morning, brightly shining (1878); Simpson, Jane
Star of peace to wanderers weary (1830, 1878); Simpson, Jane
Starry hosts are gleaming (1884); Lee, Elvira
*Steep and thorny is the way to our home (1841); Cox, Frances
Steep is the hill, and weary is the road (1864); Petre,
    Katherine
Still bright and blue doth Jordan flow (1853); Alexander, Cecil
*Still on my native shore my feet are standing (1865); Burling-
    ham, Hannah
*Still on the shores of home my feet are standing (1862); Borth-
    wick, Jane
Still, still with Thee, when purple morning breaketh (1855);
    Stowe, Harriet
*Stilly night, holy night, silent stars (1858, 1871); Elliott,
    Emily
*Strive, when thou art called of God (1855); Winkworth, Catherine
Strive, yet I do not promise (1858); Procter, Adelaide
*Suddenly to all appearing the great day of God shall come (1858);
    Cox, Elizabeth
*Sun of comfort, art Thou fled for ever (1855); Borthwick, Jane
*Sunbeams all golden (1841); Cox, Frances
*Sunk is the sun's last beam of light (1841); Cox, Frances
Sunlight of the heavenly day (1854); Waring, Anna
*Surely none like Thee can teach (1845); Fry, Henrietta
Sweet day of worship, day of rest (1870); Massey, Lucy
Sweet flowers are blooming in God's sight (1880); Stevenson,
    Matilda
Sweet hour of prayer (1861); Van Alstyne, Frances
Sweet is the scene when virtue dies (1809); Barbauld, Anna

Sweet is the solace of thy love (1850); Waring, Anna
Sweet is the work, O Lord (1829); Auber, Harriet
Sweet Shepherd, Thou has sought me (1877); Streatfeild,
    Charlotte
*Sweet slumbers now thine eyelids close (1843); Fortesque,
    Eleanor
Sweet the lesson Jesus taught (1842); Leeson, Jane
*Sweetest joy the soul can know (1858); Winkworth, Catherine
Sweetly o'er the meadows fair (1885); Hawkins, Hester

Take my life, and let it be (1874, 1878); Havergal, Frances
Take our gifts, O loving Jesus (1950); Cropper, Margaret
Take the name of Jesus with you (1870, 1871); Baxter, Lydia
Tarry with me, O my Saviour (1852, 1855); Smith, Caroline
Teach me the ways of thankfulness (1959); Lee, Dorothy
Teach me to live! (1860, 1862); Burman, Ellen
Teach me to serve Thee, Lord (1964); Phillips, Edna
Tell it out among the heathen that the Lord is King (1872);
    Havergal, Frances
Tell it out with gladness (1966); Harkness, Georgia
*Tell me not of earthly love (1862); Borthwick, Jane
Tell me the old, old story (1866); Hankey, Arabella
Tender mercies on my way (1850); Waring, Anna
Tenderly He leads us (1880); Van Alstyne, Frances
*Thank God it hath resounded (1858); Winkworth, Catherine
*Thank God, that toward eternity (1858); Winkworth, Catherine
Thanks be to God, for blessings (1946); Brown, Jeanette
*Thanks, thanks to Thee for Thy pity (1869); Warner, Anna
Thanksgiving and the voice of melody (1854); Waring, Anna
*That death is at my door (1869); Winkworth, Catherine
That mystic word of Thine, O sovereign Lord (1855); Stowe,
    Harriet
That Thou, O Lord, art ever nigh (1829); Auber, Harriet
The Advent moon shines cold and clear (1862); Rossetti,
    Christina
The angels stand around Thy throne (1848); Alexander, Cecil
The Assyrian king in splendour came (1841); Yonge, Frances
*The autumn is returning (1863); Manington, Alice
The Bible tells how sky and sea (1959); Ballard, Dorothy
The Bible tells of God's great love (1959); Doughfman, Betty
The Bible tells of God's great plan (1959); McCollough, Betty
*The blessed Cross now to us where once the Saviour bled (1858);
    Charles, Elizabeth
The breaking waves dashed high (1828); Hemans, Felicia
The changing years, eternal God (1884); Mason, Caroline
*The Child is born in Bethlehem (1858); Charles, Elizabeth
The Church and world for once (1861); Wilson, Jane
The Church of Christ has work to do (1970); Price, Marion
*The Church of Christ that He hath hallowed here (1858); Wink-
    worth, Catherine

The Church of our fathers so dear to our souls (1834); Hemans, Felicia

The churches wherever God's people are praising (1959, 1963); Ikeler, Carol

The clouds hang thick o'er Israel's camp (1885); Drane, Augusta

The clouds of night have rolled away (1903); Leefe, Isabella

*The Cross is ever good (1862); Findlater, Sarah

The Cross, the Cross, Oh that's my gain (1742); Taylor, Clare

The dawn approaches, golden streak (1869); Elliott, Charlotte

The dawn of God's dear Sabbath (1866); Cross, Ada

*The day departs, my soul and heart (1861); Borthwick, Jane

*The day expires; my soul desires (1855); Winkworth, Catherine

*The day is done, and, left alone (1863); Winkworth, Catherine

The day is done:--O God the Son (1882); Dunsterville, Patty

The day is done! the weary day of thought and toil is past (1874, 1878); Scudder, Eliza

The day is drawing nearly done (1873); Clephane, Elizabeth

*The day is gone; my soul looks on (1858); Bevan, Emma

*The day is o'er, my soul longs sore (1864); Cox, Frances

The day is slowly wending (n.d.); Rowland, May

The day of prayer is ending (1894); Armitage, Ella

The days and weeks and months pass by (1959); Lee, Dorothy

The days of old were days of night (1848); Leeson, Jane

The earth is all light and loveliness (1828); Miles, Elizabeth

The earth Thou gavest, Lord, is Thine (1961); Harkness, Georgia

The eternal gates lift up their heads (1852); Alexander, Cecil

The faithful men of every land (1848); Alexander, Cecil

The Father knows thee! learn of Him (1862); Findlater, Sarah

The floods of grief have spread around (1831); Martineau, Harriet

The flowers that bloom in the sun and shade (1881); Rossetti, Christina

The followers of the Son of God (1864); Crewdson, Jane

The glittering spangles of the sky (1740); Scott, Elizabeth

*The gloomy winter now is o'er (1869); Winkworth, Catherine

The God of heaven is pleased to see (1809); Gilbert, Ann

The golden gates are lifted up (1858); Alexander, Cecil

*The golden morn flames up the eastern sky (1858); Winkworth, Catherine

*The golden sun-beams with their joyous gleams (1855); Winkworth, Catherine

The gospel is the light (1826); Taylor, Emily

The happy days have come again (1885); Hawkins, Hester

*The happy sunshine, all is gone (1855); Winkworth, Catherine

*The holiest we enter (1847); Peters, Mary

The hours of evening close (1836); Conder, Joan

The joyful day at last is come (1870); Toke, Emma

The King of glory standeth (1867); Bancroft, Charitie

The kings of old have shrine and tomb (1829); Hemans, Felicia
The Kings of the East are riding (n.d.); Bates, Katherine
*The last days will come indeed (1841); Cox, Frances
The light that morning bringeth (1900); Dent, Caroline
The little birds fill all the air with their glee (1859);
    Charles, Elizabeth
The little birds now seek their rest (1873); Edwards, Matilda
The little cares that fretted (n.d.); Guiney, Louise
The little snowdrops rise (1880); Matheson, Annie
The Lord forgets His wonted grace (1760); Steele, Anne
*The Lord He is my Shepherd kind (1863); Manington, Alice
*The Lord is here; then let us bow before Him (1857); Dunn,
    Catherine
The Lord, my Saviour, is my Light (1760); Steele, Anne
The Lord of love will sure indulge (1769); Scott, Elizabeth
*The Lord shall come in dread of night (1858); Findlater, Sarah
The Lord, who hath redeemed our souls (1829); Auber, Harriet
The love of Christ constraining (1891); Stock, Sarah
*The love of Christ makes ever glad (1869); Klingemann, Sophie
The love that Jesus had for me (1881); Hall, Jane
The Master hath come, and He tells us to follow (1871); Doudney,
    Sarah
The Master is coming (1870); Baxter, Lydia
*The mighty Saviour comes from heaven (1841); Cox, Frances
The mourners come at break of day (1841); Adams, Sarah
The murmurs of the wilderness (1842); Peters, Mary
*The night is come, wherein at last we rest (1858); Winkworth,
    Catherine
*The old year now hath passed away (1863); Winkworth, Catherine
*The outer sunlight now is there (1873); Durand, Emily
*The precious seed of weeping (1863); Winkworth, Catherine
The red cross of our banner (1899); Thwaites, Clara
*The renewal of the world (1858); Charles, Elizabeth
The roseate hues of early dawn (1852); Alexander, Cecil
The Sabbath day has reached its close (1835); Elliott, Charlotte
The saints of god are holy men (1848); Alexander, Cecil
The saints while dispersed abroad (1842); Peters, Mary
The sands of time are sinking (1857); Cousin, Anne
*The shades of night have banished day (1857); Dunn, Catherine
The shadows of the evening hours (1862); Procter, Adelaide
The shepherds had an angel (1856); Rossetti, Christina
The sick man in his chamber (1859); Alexander, Cecil
The Son of consolation! of Levi's priestly line (1871); Coote,
    Maude
The soul's joy in God as its portion (1734, 1833); Dutton, Anne
The still small voice that speaks within (1875); Fagan, Frances
The strain of joy and gladness (1871); Coote, Maude
*The strains of joy that ceaseless flow (1872); Chester,
    Henrietta

The sun had set, the infant slept (1837); Martineau, Harriet
*The sun hath run his daily race (1843); Fortesque, Eleanor
The sun that lights yon broad blue sky (1843); Collier, Mary
*The sun's golden beams (1857); Dunn, Catherine
The sunset burns across the sky (1890); Thwaites, Clara
The tender light of home behind (1887); Stock, Sarah
The twilight softly falling (1885); Hawkins, Hester
The wanderer no more will roam (1855); Walker, Mary
*The wandering sages trace from far (1841); Cox, Frances
*The week at length is over (1863); Manington, Alice
The whole wide world for Jesus (1872); Johnson, Catherine
The wise men to Thy cradle throne (1858); Alexander, Cecil
*The woes that weigh my body down (1863); Manington, Alice
*The wonderful blessed leadings of God (1863); Manington, Alice
The world looks very beautiful (1860); Warner, Anna
*The world may fall beneath my feet (1845); Carr, Johanna
*Thee, Fount of blessing, we adore! (1858); Winkworth, Catherine
*Thee, O Immanuel, we praise (1855); Winkworth, Catherine
*Thee will I love, my strength, my tower (1863); Winkworth,
     Catherine
Their hearts shall not be moved (1842); Leeson, Jane
*Then I have conquer'd; then at last (1855); Winkworth, Catherine
*Then now at last the hour is come (1858); Winkworth, Catherine
There are many lovely things below (1871); Villiers, Margaret
There came a little child to earth (1856); Elliott, Emily
There is a bright and happy home (1885); Hawkins, Hester
There is a city bright (1898); Deck, Mary
*There is a day of rest before thee (1858); Bevan, Emma
There is a gate that stands ajar (1872, 1874); Baxter, Lydia
There is a green hill far away (1848); Alexander, Cecil
There is a happy land on high (1846); Taylor, Helen
There is a holy sacrifice (1819); Elliott, Charlotte
There is a little lonely fold (1834); Saffery, Maria
There is a noble river (1901); Clark, Bertha
There is a path that leads to God (1810); Taylor, Jane
There is a rest from sin and sorrow (1861); Maurice, Jane
There is a spot of consecrated (1839); Elliott, Charlotte
There is a vale in Israel's road (1863); Colquhoun, Frances
There is joy amongst the angels (1877); Streatfeild, Charlotte
There is life for a look at the crucified One (1860); Hull,
     Amelia
There is no cradle ready (1944); Agnew, Edith
There is no sorrow, Lord, too light (1860); Crewdson, Jane
There is one way, only one (1875); Alexander, Cecil
There seems a voice in every gale (1802); Opie, Amelia
There was a beauty on the sea (1882); Whiting, Mary
There was a lovely Garden once (1849); Bourdillon, Mary
There was a noble ark (1841); Sigourney, Lydia
There was no angel 'midst the throng (1868, 1869); Hinsdale,
     Grace

*There went three damsels ere break of day (1869); Winkworth,
    Catherine
There were ninety and nine that safely lay (1868); Clephane,
    Elizabeth
There's a cry from Macedonia (1867); Van Alstyne, Frances
There's a fight to be fought, there's a work to be done (1888);
    Stock, Sarah
There's a fold, both safe and happy (1878, 1880); Black, Mary
They are gathering homeward from every land (1861); Leslie,
    Mary
They are waiting everywhere (1893); Stock, Sarah
They come and go, the seasons fair (1891); Elliott, Emily
Thine for ever, God of love (1847, 1848); Maude, Mary
Thine, most gracious Lord (n.d.); Hawks, Annie
*Think, O my soul, that whilst thou art (1843); Fortesque,
    Eleanor
Think of Jesus in the morning (1900); Lancaster, Mary
Think on the mercy of our God (1834, 1841); Garnier, Mary
Think upon Eve and Adam's sin (1835); Mozley, Harriet
This day let grateful praise ascend (1840); Hale, Mary
*This day sent forth His heralds bold (1867); Cox, Frances
This day the Lord has spoken (1890); Marston, Annie
This healthful mystery (1884); Hernaman, Claudia
*This holy feast, by Jesus spread (1863); Cox, Frances
This is a precious book indeed (1809); Taylor, Jane
This is enough; although 'twere sweet (1834); Elliott,
    Charlotte
This is God's holy house (1950); Oglevee, Louise
This is God's most holy day (n.d.); Parson, Elizabeth
This is our prayer, dear God (1942); Drury, Miriam
*This is the day the Lord hath made (1864); Borthwick, Jane
This is the day to tune with care (1839); Elliott, Charlotte
This is the day when Jesus Christ (1870); Toke, Emma
This is the moment where Christ's disciples see (1839); Elliott,
    Charlotte
*This life is like a flying dream (1858); Findlater, Sarah
*This year is just going away (1810); Gilbert, Ann
*Tho' all men's faith had banished (1841); Lowe, Helen
*Thou All-sufficient One! Who art (1858); Warner, Anna
*Thou art coming, O my Saviour (1873); Havergal, Frances
*Thou art first and best (1869); Winkworth, Catherine
Thou art gone up on high (1851, 1852); Toke, Emma
Thou art in Zion laid (1825, 1830); Bulmer, Agnes
Thou art my Shepherd (1866); Haycraft, Margaret
Thou art, O God, the God of might (1921); Perkins, Emily
Thou art the way, O Lord (1873); Taylor, Rebekah
Thou art with me, O my Father (n.d.); Saxby, Jane
Thou bidd'st us to seek Thee early (1873); Threlfall, Jeannette
*Thou burning love, Thou holy flame (1869); Winkworth,
    Catherine

Thou, by whose strength the mountains stand (1829); Auber,
    Harriet
*Thou deep abyss of blessed love (1858); Charles, Elizabeth
Thou didst leave Thy throne and Thy kingly crown (1864);
    Elliott, Emily
*Thou eternal life bestowest (1864); Borthwick, Jane
*Thou fairest child divine (1858); Winkworth, Catherine
*Thou fathomless abyss of love (1869); Winkworth, Catherine
Thou glorious Sun of righteousness (1839); Elliott, Charlotte
Thou God of love, beneath Thy sheltering wings (1849); Saxby,
    Jane
*Thou good and gracious God (1864); Cox, Frances
Thou grave divine, encircling all (1852, 1857); Scudder, Eliza
Thou, Guardian of my earliest days (1836); Thrupp, Dorothy
*Thou hast borne our sins and sorrows (1875); Borthwick, Jane
Thou hast gone up again (1880); Scudder, Eliza
*Thou heavenly Lord of light (1869); Winkworth, Catherine
*Thou holiest love, whom most I love (1855); Winkworth,
    Catherine
*Thou holiest Saviour, sacred spring (1857); Dunn, Catherine
*Thou, Jesu, art my consolation (1866); Burlingham, Hannah
Thou long disowned, reviled, opprest (1864); Scudder, Eliza
*Thou love may weep with breaking heart (1858); Winkworth,
    Catherine
Thou must go forth alone, my soul (1845); Jevon, Mary
*Thou shalt rise! my dust thou shalt arise (1855); Borthwick,
    Jane
Thou soft flowing Kedron, by thy silver stream (1791); DeFleury,
    Maria
*Thou, solemn ocean, rollest to the strand (n.d.); Winkworth,
    Catherine
Thou stand'st between the earth and heaven (1867, 1869);
    Hinsdale, Grace
*Thou sweet beloved will of God (1858); Bevan, Emma
*Thou treasure of all treasures (1863); Manington, Alice
*Thou virgin soul! O thou (1863); Winkworth, Catherine
*Thou weepest o'er, Jerusalem (1855); Winkworth, Catherine
*Thou who breakest every chain (1858); Winkworth, Catherine
*Thou who breakest every fetter (1858); Bevan, Emma
Thou who didst for Peter's faith (1812); Gilbert, Ann
Thou who didst stoop below (1827); Miles, Elizabeth
Thou who hero-like hast striven (1862); Drane, Augusta
Thou who with dying lips (1878); Wiglesworth, Esther
*Thou who'rt One, and yet as three (1863); Manington, Alice
*Though all to Thee were faithless (1855); Winkworth, Catherine
Though gloom may veil our troubled skies (1864); Crewdson, Jane
Though home be dear, and life be sweet (1894); Armitage, Ella
Though some good things of lower worth (1850); Waring, Anna

*Thou'rt mine, yet, still Thou'rt mine own (1858); Winkworth, Catherine
*Thrice happy he who serveth (1865); Burlingham, Hannah
 Through the love of God our Saviour (1847); Peters, Mary
 Through the yesterday of ages (1876, 1878); Havergal, Frances
*Throw, soul, I say, thy fears away (1864); Manington, Alice
*Throw the glorious gates wide open (1863); Manington, Alice
*Thus said the Lord--thy days of health are over (1858); Borthwick, Jane
 Thus shalt thou love the Almighty God (1826); Taylor, Emily
*Thus, step by step, my journey to the Infinite (1873); Durand, Emily
*Thus, then another year of pilgrim-life (1873); Durand, Emily
 Thy bounties, gracious Lord (1740); Scott, Elizabeth
 Thy courts, O Lord, are open (1883); Headlam, Margaret
 Thy grace, O Lord, to us hath shown (1847); Peters, Mary
 Thy kingdom come; yea, bid it come (1885); Tynan-Hinkson, Katharine
 Thy little one, O Saviour dear (1885); Hawkins, Hester
*Thy mercy, Lord, is still the same (1843); Fortesque, Eleanor
*Thy parent's arms now yield thee (1858); Winkworth, Catherine
 Thy servants, Lord, are dear to Thee (n.d.); Stock, Sarah
 Thy will be done, I will not fear (1843); Hornblower, Jane
*Thy word, O Lord, like gentle dews (1855); Winkworth, Catherine
*Till the thirty years were finished (1867); Charles, Elizabeth
 Time is swiftly passing o'er us (1882); Whiting, Mary
*Time, thou speedest on but slowly (1855); Winkworth, Catherine
*Times are changing, days are flying (1859); Borthwick, Jane
 'Tis good, O Jesu, that alone with Thee (n.d.); Wilson, Jane
 'Tis not the Cross I have to bear (1864); Crewdson, Jane
 'Tis religion that can give (1755); Masters, Mary
 'Tis so sweet to trust in Jesus (n.d.); Stead, Louisa
*'Tis spring, the time of singing (1866); Burlingham, Hannah
 'Tis the blessed hour of prayer (1880); Van Alstyne, Frances
 'Tis the great Father we adore (1817, 1828); Saffery, Maria
*To Barnabas, Thy servant blest (1872); Chester, Henrietta
*To God alone in the highest heaven (1845); Fry, Henrietta
 To God be the glory, great things He hath done (1875); Van Alstyne, Frances
*To God's all-gracious heart and mind (1869); Winkworth, Catherine
 To heaven our longing eyes we raise (1829); Auber, Harriet
 To Him who is the Life of life (1866); Cary, Alice
 To mourn our dead we gather here (1903); Whiting, Mary
 To the work, to the work (1871); Van Alstyne, Frances
 To Thee, and to Thy Christ, O God (1876); Cousin, Anne
 To Thee, Creator, in whose love (1882); Whiting, Mary
 To Thee, my God, to Thee (1845); Carpenter, Mary

To Thee, O Comforter divine (1872, 18/4); Havergal, Frances
*To Thee, O Lord, I come with singing (1866); Burlingham,
   Hannah
To Thee, the giver of all good (1885); Hawkins, Hester
*To Thee, Thou Holy Spirit, now (1845); Fry, Henrietta
To thy father and thy mother (1876); Cousin, Anne Ross
*To-day mine, to-morrow Thine (1858); Warner, Anna
*To-day our Lord went upon high (1858); Winkworth, Catherine
Toiling in the path of duty (1882); Clephane, Anna
Toss'd with rough winds, and faint with fear (1859); Charles,
   Elizabeth
*Treasure beyond all treasure (1857); Dunn, Catherine
Treasures we have gathered here (1896); Stock, Sarah
*Trembling, I rejoice (1869); Winkworth, Catherine
True friends help each other (1876); Baker, Amy
*True mirrour of the Godhead: perfect light (1858); Winkworth,
   Catherine
*True Shepherd, who in love most deep (1863); Winkworth, Cath-
   erine
True-hearted, whole-hearted, faithful and loyal (1878); Havergal,
   Frances
Truly the light of morn is sweet (1826); Taylor, Emily
'Twill not be long--our journey here (1868); Van Alstyne,
   Frances

Under Thy wings, my God, I rest (1850); Waring, Anna
Unfurl the Christian standard with firm and fearless hand
   (1872, 1874); Havergal, Frances
Unto him that hath Thou givest (1876); Havergal, Frances
Unto Him whose name is holy (1866); Elliott, Emily
Unwearied with earthly toil and care (1843); Gilbert, Ann
Unworthy is thanksgiving (1847); Peters, Mary
*Up! Christian! gird thee to the strife (1865); Burlingham,
   Hannah
*Up! Christian man, and join the fight (1863); Manington, Alice
Up in heaven, up in heaven (1848); Alexander, Cecil
*Up! yes upward to Thy gladness rise (1858); Winkworth,
   Catherine
Upon this sad and solemn day (1870); Toke, Emma
*Upwards, upwards to Thy gladness (1857); Dunn, Catherine

Vainly through night's weary hours (1829); Auber, Harriet
Vainly through the night the danger (1829); Auber, Harriet
*Voices of spring, with what gladness I hear you again (1862);
   Borthwick, Jane

*Wail ye not, but requiems sing (1842); Leeson, Jane
*Wake, awake, for night is flying (1858); Winkworth, Catherine

*Wake hearts devout whom love inspires (1872); Chester, Henrietta
 Wake the song, O Zion's daughter (n.d.); Leeson, Jane
*Wake! the startling watch-cry pealeth (1864); Cox, Frances
*Wake! the welcome day appeareth (1841); Cox, Frances
*Wake up, my heart, the night has flown (1863); Manington, Alice
 Wake, ye saints, the song of triumph (1861, 1864); Leeson, Jane
*Waken! from the tower it soundeth (1858); Bevan, Emma
 Walking with Jesus day by day (1894); Lancaster, Mary
*We all believe in one true God (1863); Winkworth, Catherine
 We are but little children poor (1850); Alexander, Cecil
 We are children of the King (1891); Stock, Sarah
 We are going, we are going (1864); Van Alstyne, Frances
 We are little Christian children (1848); Alexander, Cecil
 We are marching on with shield and banner bright (1867); Van
    Alstyne, Frances
 We are not left to walk alone (1855); Walker, Mary
 We are only little workers (1876); Baker, Amy
 We are so happy, God's own little flock (n.d.); Johnson,
    Catherine
*We are the Lord's!--in life, in death remaining (1862); Find-
    later, Sarah
*We are the Lord's in living or in dying (1859); Fry, Henrietta
 We ask for peace, O Lord (1858); Procter, Adelaide
*We believe in one true God, Father, Son, and Holy Ghost (1863);
    Winkworth, Catherine
 We bless Thee for this sacred day (1820); Gilman, Caroline
 We bless Thee, Lord, for that clear light (1870); Toke, Emma
 We bring no glittering treasures (1848, 1849); Phillips, Harriet
*We Christians may rejoice to-day (1863); Winkworth, Catherine
 We come, O Christ, to Thee (1946, 1948); Clarkson, Edith
 We come, O Lord, before Thy throne (1836); Brown, Phoebe
*We come, our hearts with gladness glowing (1841); Cox, Frances
 We cry to Thee, O Jesu (1861); Wilson, Jane
 We gather here to sing to God (1960); Duckert, Mary
 We hail renouned Alban (1861); Wilson, Jane
 We have heard a joyful sound (1898); Owens, Priscilla
 We have no tears Thou wilt not dry (1864); Kimball, Harriet
 We have not seen Thy footsteps tread (1841); Richter, Anne
 We know not a voice of that river (1892); Rossetti, Christina
 We know not how the rays that stream (1868); Stock, Sarah
 We know there's a bright and glorious home (1865); Wilson,
    Margaret
 We love Thee, Lord, yet not alone (1835); Elliott, Julia
 We meet, we part, how few the hours! (1880); Wills, Ruth
 We mourn for those who toil (1831); Sigourney, Lydia
*We plough the fields, and scatter (1861); Campbell, Jane
*We praise and bless Thee, gracious Lord (1855); Borthwick, Jane
 We praise our Lord to-day (1871); Doudney, Sarah

We praise Thee if one rescued soul (1846); Sigourney, Lydia
We praise Thee in the morning (1873); Threlfall, Jeannette
We praise Thee, O God our Redeemer, Creator (1902); Cory, Julia
We praise Thee, we bless Thee (1857); Strafford, Elizabeth
*We read that to Isaiah it befel (1845); Fry, Henrietta
We shall have a new name in that land (1881); Hall, Jane
We shall see Him, in our nature (1847); Pyper, Mary
We shall sleep, but not forever (1878); Kidder, Mary
We sing a loving Jesus (1871); Doudney, Sarah
*We sing to Thee, Emmanuel, the Prince (1864); Cox, Frances
We speak of the realms of the blest (1829); Mills, Elizabeth
We thank Thee, Father, for the day (1850); Sigourney, Lydia
We thank Thee, God, for eyes to see (1936); Brown, Jeanette
We thank Thee, God, our Father (1943); McCaw, Mabel
We thank Thee, Lord, for all Thy gifts (1935); Ferguson, Jessie
We, Thy people, praise Thee, praise Thee (n.d.); Page, Kate
*We were washed in holy water (1848); Alexander, Cecil
*Wearily my spirit speaketh (1858); Bevan, Emma
*Weary heart, be not desponding (1873); Durand, Emily
*Weary, waiting to depart (1855); Findlater, Sarah
*Weep not,--Jesus lives on high (1854); Findlater, Sarah
*Welcome, Thou victor in the strife (1855); Winkworth, Catherine
Welcome to me, the darkest night (1835); Elliott, Julia
Welcome, ye hopeful heirs of heaven (1824); Brown, Phoebe
We're pilgrims in the wilderness (1847); Peters, Mary
What a strange and wondrous story (1836); Thrupp, Dorothy
What are these that glow from afar? (1865); Rossetti, Christina
What blissful harmonies above (1836); Codner, Joan
*What God decrees, child of His love (1858); Findlater, Sarah
*What God does is done aright (1872); Chester, Henrietta
*What God does, that is rightly done (1864); Borthwick, Jane
*What God hath done is done aright (1864); Cox, Frances
*What had I been, if Thou wert not (1855); Winkworth, Catherine
What hast Thou done for me (1877, 1879); Havergal, Frances
What hope was Thine, O Christ (1831); Martineau, Harriet
What is the name of the Lord God Almighty? (1905); Matheson,
    Annie
What is there, Lord, a child can do? (n.d.); Taylor, Jane
*What is this that round the throne (1869); Warner, Anna
What know we, Holy God, of Thee? (1872); Havergal, Frances
*What laws, my blessed Saviour, hast Thou broken (1864); Cox,
    Frances
What led the Son of God? (1830); Thrupp, Dorothy
What marks the dawning of the year? (1859); Charles, Elizabeth
What means this eager, anxious throng (1863); Campbell, Etta
*What might I not have been without Thee (1841); Lowe, Helen
*What no human eye hath seen (1855); Borthwick, Jane
*What pleases God, O pious soul (1858); Winkworth, Catherine

*What pleaseth God with joy receive (1857); Dunn, Catherine
 What praise unto the Lamb is due (n.d.); Taylor, Clare
*What shall I, a sinner, do? (1863); Winkworth, Catherine
*What shall I be? my Lord, when I behold Thee (1855); Findlater,
     Sarah
 What was the holy joy, O Lord (1882); Whiting, Mary
*What within me and without (1855); Winkworth, Catherine
*Whate'er my God ordains is right (1858); Winkworth, Catherine
*Whate'er of beauty I behold (1843); Fortesque, Eleanor
 Whatever dims the sense of truth (1840); Hale, Mary
*Whatever God does is well (1858); Warner, Anna
 When Abram full of sacred awe (1769); Scott, Elizabeth
 When adverse winds and waves arise (1823); Sigourney, Lydia
*When affliction rends the heart (1843); Fortesque, Eleanor
*When afflictions sore oppress you (1841); Cox, Frances
 When all bespeaks a father's love (1829); Auber, Harriet
*When anguish'd and perplexed (1858); Winkworth, Catherine
 When as returns the solemn day (1807); Barbauld, Anna
 When blooming youth is snatched away (1760); Steele, Anne
 When daily I kneel down to pray (1809); Taylor, Jane
 When dangers press and fears evade (1829); Auber, Harriet
 When for some little insult given (1809); Taylor, Jane
 When from Egypt's house of bondage (1873); Threlfall, Jeannette
 When human hopes and joys depart (1820); Jevon, Mary
*When I, Creator, view Thy might (1863); Manington, Alice
 When I listen to Thy word (n.d.); Gilbert, Ann
 When I resolved to watch my thoughts (1760); Steele, Anne
 When I survey life's varied scene (1760); Steele, Anne
 When in silence o'er the deep (1844); Hale, Mary
*When in the hour of utmost need (1858); Winkworth, Catherine
*When in thine hours of grief (1843); Fortesque, Eleanor
 When Jesus comes to reward His servants (1876); Van Alstyne,
     Frances
 When Jesus' friend had ceased to be; Browning, Elizabeth
 When Jesus saw the fishermen (1953); Agnew, Edith
 When Jesus taught the word of God (1961); Clarke, Sara
 When Jesus was on earth He used (1862); Clare, Mary
 When life as opening buds is sweet (1814); Barbauld, Anna
 When little Samuel woke (1809); Gilbert, Ann
 When Mary to the Heavenly Guest (1836); Conder, Joan
*When my last hour is close at hand (1863); Winkworth, Catherine
 When mysterious whispers are floating about (1864); Hearn,
     Marianne
*When o'er my sins I sorrow (1863); Winkworth, Catherine
 When of old the Jewish mothers (1853); Alexander, Cecil
 When on devotion's seraph wing (1828); Miles, Elizabeth
*When on the Cross the Saviour hung (1863); Winkworth, Catherine
*When, only dearest Lord, I prove (1857); Dunn, Catherine

When safely on dry land once more (1835); Mozley, Harriet
When Samuel heard, in still mid-night (1831); Martineau,
     Harriet
When silent steal across my soul (1857); Torrey, Mary
*When sorrow and remorse (1855); Winkworth, Catherine
 When summer suns their radiance fling (1826); Taylor, Emily
 When the churchyard side by side (1848); Alexander, Cecil
 When the disciples saw their Lord (1838); Opie, Amelia
*When the last agony draws nigh (1855); Winkworth, Catherine
*When the Lord recalls the banish'd (1858); Winkworth, Catherine
 When the parting bosom bleeds (1846); Sigourney, Lydia
 When there is peace (1905); Matheson, Annie
*When these brief trial-days are spent (1869); Winkworth,
     Catherine
 When through life's dewy fields we go (1880); Matheson, Annie
 When to the house of God we go (1809); Taylor, Jane
 When waves of trouble round me swell (1834); Elliott, Charlotte
 When we hear Scripture read in church (1960); Duckert, Mary
 When we in holy worship (1878); Wiglesworth, Esther
 When we reach our peaceful dwelling (1876); Cousin, Anne
*When we walk the paths of life (1845); Fry, Henrietta
 When winds are raging o'er the upper ocean (1855); Stowe,
     Harriet
 When wounded sore the stricken soul (1858); Alexander, Cecil
 Whence these sorrows, Saviour, say? (1827); Herschell, Esther
*Whene'er again, thou sinkest (1858); Winkworth, Catherine
 Where is the tree the prophet threw (1828); Hemans, Felicia
*Where the lambs sleep, there shepherds watch around (1862);
     Findlater, Sarah
*Where wilt thou go? (1863); Manington, Alice
 Where wilt thou put thy trust? (1845); Sigourney, Lydia
*Where'er I go, whate'er my task (1858); Winkworth, Catherine
 Where'er the Lord shall build my house (1740); Scott, Elizabeth
*Wherefore dost thou longer tarry (1858); Winkworth, Catherine
*Wherefore should I grieve and pine (1858); Winkworth, Catherine
 Wherever people live in love (1959); Fritz, Dorothy
 While justice waves her vengeful hand (1757, 1760); Steele,
     Anne
*While on earth, dear Lord, I roam (1857); Dunn, Catherine
 While Thee I seek, protecting power (1786); Williams, Helen
*While yet the morn is breaking (1863); Winkworth, Catherine
 Whiteness of the winter's snow (1905); Butler, Mary
*Whither, oh whither?--with blindfolded eyes (1858); Borthwick,
     Jane
*Whither shall we flee (1857); Dunn, Catherine
*Who are these like stars appearing? (1841); Cox, Frances
 Who are they in heaven who stand? (1846); Thrupp, Dorothy
*Who are those before God's throne (1855); Winkworth, Catherine

*Who are those round God's throne standing (1863); Manington,
    Alice
Who can condemn, since Christ hath died? (1742); Taylor, Clare
*Who can my soul from Jesus sever (1863); Manington, Alice
Who climbeth up too high (1872); Clephane, Elizabeth
Who is on the Lord's side? (1877, 1879); Havergal, Frances
*Who keepeth not God's word, yet saith (1858); Winkworth,
    Catherine
*Who knows how near my end may be? (1858); Winkworth, Catherine
Who, O Lord, when life is o'er (1829); Auber, Harriet
*Who puts his trust in God most just (1858); Winkworth, Catherine
*Who seeks in weakness an excuse (1855); Winkworth, Catherine
Who shall behold the King of kings (1826); Taylor, Emily
Who that o'er many a barren part (1826); Taylor, Emily
Who, when darkness gathered o'er us (1832); Gould, Hannah
*Who would make the prize his own (1858); Winkworth, Catherine
Whom have we, Lord, but Thee (1842); Peters, Mary
Whom have we, Lord, in heaven but Thee (1829); Auber, Harriet
*Whom Jesus loves (1883); Spaeth, Mrs. H.R.
Wide, ye heavenly gates, unfold (1829); Auber, Harriet
While all the golden harps above (1829); Auber, Harriet
*Why art thou thus cast down, my heart (1858); Winkworth,
    Catherine
*Why haltest thus, deluded heart (1855); Winkworth, Catherine
*Why is it that life is no longer sad? (1869); Cox, Frances
Why labour for treasures that rust and decay? (1871); Van Alstyne,
    Frances
Why lived I not in those blest days? (1841); Yonge, Charlotte
Why, O my heart, these anxious cares (1769); Scott, Elizabeth
Why perish with the cold and with hunger? (1881); Baker, Mary
Why should we weep for those who die (1843); Gilbert, Ann
*Why this sad and mournful guise (1857); Dunn, Catherine
Why weepest Thou? (n.d.); Hawks, Annie
Will God who made the earth and sea (1839); Follen, Elizabeth
*Will that not joyful be? (1854); Findlater, Sarah
Will ye flee in danger's hour (1827); Colquhoun, Frances
Will ye not come to Him for life? (1873); Havergal, Frances
Will your anchor hold in the storms of life? (n.d.); Owens,
    Priscilla
Wilt Thou hear the voice of praise (n.d.); Rice, Caroline
*Wilt Thou not, my Shepherd true (1841); Cox, Frances
*With brighter glory, Easter sun (1873); Durand, Emily
With hearts in love abounding (1829); Auber, Harriet
With joy we hail the sacred day (1829); Auber, Harriet
*With peace and joy from earth I go (1845); Fry, Henrietta
With quivering heart and trembling will (1866); Havergal,
    Frances
*With sorrow now for past misdeed (1864); Cox, Frances

With tearful eyes I look around (1835); Elliott, Charlotte
*With tears o'er lost Jerusalem (1841); Cox, Frances
With thankful hearts, we meet, O Lord (1842); Peters, Mary
*With the glow of ardent longing (1865); Burlingham, Hannah
With voice of joy and singing (1887); Stock, Sarah
*Within a Garden's bound (1864); Cox, Frances
Within the Church's hallowed walls (1969); Drury, Miriam
*Word by God the Father spoken (1863); Manington, Alice
Work and never weary (1868); Miller, Emily
Work for the night is coming (1854); Coghill, Annie
World around us, sky above us (1970); Garriott, Jean
*World farewell, my soul is weary (1857); Dunn, Catherine
*World, farewell! of thee I'm tired (1858); Winkworth, Catherine
Worthy of all adoration (1867, 1869); Havergal, Frances
*Worthy of praise, the Master-hand (1869); Winkworth, Catherine
*Wouldst thou inherit life with Christ on high? (1855); Wink-
     worth, Catherine
*Wouldst thou, my soul, the secret find (1843); Fortesque,
     Eleanor
*Wrestle on! for God is pleading (1865); Burlingham, Hannah

 Ye angels who stand round the throne (1791); DeFleury, Maria
*Ye heavens, O hast your dews to shed (1858); Winkworth, Catherin
*Ye messengers of Christ (1859); Fry, Henrietta
*Ye servants of the Lord, who stand (1863); Winkworth, Catherine
*Ye sons of men, in earnest (1863); Winkworth, Catherine
 Ye who hear the blessed call (1869); Havergal, Frances
 Ye wretched, hungry, starving poor (1760); Steele, Anne
*Yea, my spirit fain would sink (1855); Winkworth, Catherine
 Yes, He knows the way is dreary (1865, 1867); Havergal, Frances
*Yes! it shall be well at morning (1862); Findlater, Sarah
*Yes! our Shepherd leads with gentle hand (1854); Borthwick,
     Jane
*Yes, still for us a rest remaineth (1869); Borthwick, Jane
*Yes, there remaineth yet a rest (1855); Winkworth, Catherine
*Yesterday the happy earth (1858); Charles, Elizabeth
 Yet a little while (1830, 1831); Cockburn-Campbell, Margaret
 Young children once to Jesus came (1810); Taylor, Jane
 Youthful, weak, and unprotected (1858); Parson, Elizabeth